REFORMED BY BISHOPS

Galloway, Orkney and Caithness

Gordon Donaldson

The Edina Press
Edinburgh

THE EDINA PRESS

24 York Place
Edinburgh

First published 1987

ISBN   0   905695   12   7

Printed in Scotland
by
Office Printing Services, Edinburgh EH3 7BJ.

CONTENTS

PREFACE

Almost as far back as I can remember, I have been a strong advocate of local studies, if only on the elementary ground that it is dangerous to generalise and hazardous to pronounce on what was happening throughout the country as a whole unless one knows what was happening in the localities. Yet my investigations into regional aspects of reformation history started and progressed quite fortuitously and it was only by chance that three of my compositions fell into some kind of pattern. It all began very indirectly — and somewhat incredibly it must seem — because in 1938 the present parish church of South Yell had its centenary. The local minister, the Rev. Douglas Beck, and I collaborated in producing an account of a hundred years of history, published in the *Shetland Times* in December 1938. It occurred to me that as part of the commemoration there should be erected in the church a tablet with the names of the men who had ministered in the parish since the reformation. I prepared the list on the basis of what appeared in the *Fasti Ecclesiae Scoticanae*, for at that time I did not know any better. However, once I joined the Register House staff and began to look at the records, I discovered that the *Fasti* has its imperfections and in particular that my list began by repeating a howler. I was thus led on to my first published essay in Scottish reformation studies, in articles on 'The Early Ministers of the North Isles' — that is, Yell, Unst and Fetlar — published in the *Shetland News* in September-October 1943. I followed those with another series of newspaper articles, this time on 'The Archdeaconry of Shetland in the Sixteenth Century' (*Shetland News*, 1946), which covered the parish of Tingwall and contained a note on Nesting. I put material together in those same years on the remaining Shetland parishes, but this work remained unpublished until 1985, when an article on 'Some Shetland Parishes at the Reformation' appeared in *Essays in Shetland History* (ed. Barbara E. Crawford). However, my investigations of Shetland clergy had led me on to do an article in 1960 on 'Bishop Adam Bothwell and the Reformation in Orkney' in *Records of the Scottish Church History Society*, xiii.

I had not finished my searches on Shetland parishes before my attention was drawn or directed to the other end of the country, namely Galloway, and the stimulus came from that energetic and persuasive man, the late Dr. R.C. Reid, who was always on the lookout for contributions to the Dumfriesshire and Galloway Natural History and Antiquarian Society's *Transactions*. To satisfy him I undertook first an article on 'Alexander Gordon, Bishop of Galloway' and later one on 'The Galloway Clergy at the Reformation' (1947 and 1953).

At some remote date which I cannot now determine, I was pressed somewhat similarly, but less productively, into studying the reformation in Perthshire. I did give a talk to a society in Perth and prepared a version for publication, but the project seemed to collapse and this piece of work never saw the light of day. Then in 1960, when there was a good deal of commemoration of the 'Quatercentenary of the Reformation', I gave a talk to the Old Edinburgh Club on the Reformation in Edinburgh — not forgetting Leith, which had such a reputation for godliness in the sixteenth century. And I accepted an invitation to give a talk in Linlithgow on the Reformation in West Lothian.

This had all been very haphazard. But I had seen enough to learn that the pattern varied from district to district and I thought it likely that one factor in shaping the progress of the reformation in any area would be the extent to which some kind of leadership encouraged or discouraged the expansion of the reformed ministry and the participation of the existing clergy in the work of the reformed church. Now, the dioceses of Orkney and Galloway both had bishops who supported the reformation and I had noticed that they took responsibility for establishing the new church organisation in their dioceses. Forty years ago, in an article in the *English Historical Review* on 'The Scottish Episcopate at the Reformation' (vol. lx), I indicated my awareness of a third active reforming bishop, Robert Stewart of Caithness. I did not turn my attention seriously to him until quite recently, simply because there was nothing to draw me to an interest in Caithness and no one to encourage me to study it, though when I was on the Register House staff and preparing an inventory of the Mey Papers I kept notes of material on the bishop. From time to time, however, I have drawn attention to the trio of conforming bishops, and I took a malicious pleasure in observing that their work disproved the statement in the act of 1690 abolishing 'prelacy' that 'prelacy and the superiority of any office in the Church above presbyters is and hath been a great and unsupportable grievance to this nation and contrary to the inclinations of the generality of the people ever since the Reformation, *they having reformed from popery by presbyters*'.

That final phrase enshrines one of the many cherished delusions of the Scots. Such delusions can so dominate the mind that it is closed to the truth, however frequently and plainly the truth is set forth. No doubt this explains why, despite the work that had been done, by me and others, on the reformation in various areas, a writer in 1983 could bring herself to say that 'local reformation studies have scarcely begun in Scotland' and that 'the first step in this direction was taken' in a pamphlet published so late as 1978.[1] The fact that articles have been disregarded or ignored may justify their re-presentation in a book.

1   Norman Macdougall (ed.), *Church, Politics and Society*, 66,80.

ABBREVIATIONS

A & D	Acts and Decreets of the Court of Session (SRO)
APS	*Acts of the Parliaments of Scotland*
BUK	*Acts and Proceedings of the General Assemblies*
CSP Scot.	*Calendar of State Papers relating to Scotland and Mary, Queen of Scots*
CSP For.	*Calendar of State Papers, Foreign Series*
Calderwood	David Calderwood, *History of the Church of Scotland* (Wodrow Society)
DNB	*Dictionary of National Biography*
ER	*Exchequer Rolls of Scotland*
EUL	Edinburgh University Library
HMC	Historical Manuscripts Commission
IR	*Innes Review*
Knox	John Knox, *History of the Reformation*, ed. Dickinson
L & P	*Letters and Papers, Foreign and Domestic, of the reign of Henry VIII*
NLS	National Library of Scotland
OP	*Originales Parochiales Scotiae*
Pitcairn	Pitcairn, *Criminal Trials*
Public Affairs	*Acts of the Lords of Council in Public Affairs*
PSAS	*Proceedings of the Society of Antiquaries of Scotland*
REO	*Records of the Earldom of Orkney* (SHS)
RMS	*Register of the Great Seal of Scotland*
RPC	*Register of the Privy Council of Scotland*
RSS	*Register of the Privy Seal of Scotland*
Reg. Pres.	Register of Presentations to Benefices (SRO)
SHS	Scottish History Society
SRO	Scottish Record Office
SRS	Scottish Record Society
TA	*Accounts of the Treasurers of Scotland*
TB	*Accounts of the Collectors of Thirds of Benefices* (SHS)
TDGNHAS	*Transactions of the Dumfriesshire and Galloway Natural History and Antiquarian Society*

INTRODUCTION

In August 1560 a Scottish parliament adopted a reformed Confession of Faith, abrogated papal authority and forbade the celebration of Mass, but nothing was said about how the reformed church was to be organised. In practice the only institutions which existed were some local congregations, who elected their ministers, elders and deacons. No general arrangements had been made for the oversight of ministers, and, so far as the evidence shows, there was no regional organisation. Above that level there was only minimal direction from a central authority of some kind — in the summer of 1560 a meeting of 'the commissioners of burghs, and some of the nobility and barons', in December 1560 a gathering of half-a-dozen ministers and about three dozen laymen, styled 'commissioners of kirks', and early in 1561 the privy council (that is, the organ of the protestant lords who operated a kind of provisional government until Queen Mary returned from France in August). It is impossible to discern a regular general assembly before 1562.

When the reformers did put forward, in a Book of Discipline which took its final shape in January 1561, their plans for the organisation and endowment of their church, they acknowledged the need for a rank of clergy who should have the oversight of inferior ministers, and proposed to commit essential functions in the admission and supervision of parochial clergy (usually thought of as episcopal duties), to ten superintendents, each responsible for a diocese containing about a hundred parishes. The Book of Discipline, however, did not obtain the approval of parliament, which alone could have put its financial proposals into effect, and instead the entire structure of the old régime remained intact: all the existing clergy, from bishops downwards, continued to draw their revenues, subject only in most cases to the deduction of one third, which was collected partly to augment the revenues of the crown and partly to pay stipends to the men who were to provide reformed services in the parishes. At various dates from March 1561 onwards superintendents were appointed to five of the ten dioceses whose boundaries were defined in the Book of Discipline, where they performed the administrative and judicial functions previously carried out by bishops. They took the leading part in the admission of ministers, supervised them and exercised discipline over them; with the kirk session of the chief town of his diocese a superintendent constituted a court with competence in some of the traditional fields of ecclesiastical jurisdiction; he presided over diocesan synods; and, along with ministers of his choice, attended general assemblies. No more superintendents beyond the original five were ever appointed, partly because the reformed church, in straitened financial circumstances, could not afford their salaries, which were in the range £500-£700 annually. It was cheaper to employ parish ministers as 'commissioners' to carry out at least some of the duties of superintendents on a part-time basis, for they required only £100-£200, in addition to their parochial stipends.

There arose the question of the possible value to the reformed church of those bishops who supported it. Parliament had merely forbidden bishops to exercise those powers which they possessed by papal authority, and in practice bishops continued, quite legally, to give admission to benefices and even to exercise some of their judicial functions. Only two of the eleven bishops in office could be regarded as conscientious papalists; five occupied a less committed position, generally conservative but not wholly hostile to the reformed church; and four — Alexander Gordon of Galloway, Adam Bothwell of Orkney, Robert Stewart of Caithness and James Hamilton of Argyll — supported the reformation. Now, John Knox had laid down that a bishop who receives profit and feeds not the flock by his own labours is a thief and a murderer, and the implication was that a bishop who received profit had a right and a duty to feed the flock. The argument would run like this: there is episcopal work to be done in the church; there are no funds to pay superintendents to do it, but there are men receiving episcopal revenues, professing the reformed faith and legally entitled to exercise certain episcopal functions — why should not they serve as superintendents? Any such reasoning apart, it would not have been surprising if, in the absence in 1560 of any direction or instructions from the centre, it was assumed in some areas, perhaps especially in remote areas, that the bishops would simply go on exercising their traditional functions, and this is what happened. Bishops continued their accustomed work without seeking or receiving any fresh authorisation. This is apparent from the careers of at least Gordon and Bothwell, and a resolution of the general assembly of December 1562 indicates that bishops had been exercising their functions without authorisation from the assembly: 'inhibition shall be made to all and sundry now serving in the ministry ... that has not been presented by the people or a part thereof to the superintendent and he, after examination and trial, has not appointed them to their charges; and *this act to have strength against them that are called bishops* as others pretending to any ministry within the kirk'.[1] The first known act of the general assembly explicitly recognising the place of the reformed bishops in the church came six months later, when three of them were authorised to act as overseers of their dioceses.

From time to time in later years the assembly renewed its commission to the bishops, but the evidence for what they actually did in their dioceses, as distinct from what they were expected to do, comes less from the *Acts and Proceedings of the General Assemblies* than from a number of other sources. Our knowledge of the movements of the bishops, especially of the time they spent in their dioceses, derives largely from charters and other deeds issued by them. The *Accounts of the*

Collectors of Thirds of Benefices record the payments and allowances made to them in respect of their labours in the interests of the reformed church, and these accounts are also a mine of information about the way in which existing clergy accepted the reformation and the stages by which the reformed ministry expanded in each diocese under the direction of the bishops. It is not only these Accounts which give us details about the clergy, for there is a *Register of Ministers, Exhorters and Readers and their Stipends*, begun in 1567 and kept up to date by amendments until 1573, and casual references to individual clergy turn up in charters, deeds, records of judicial proceedings, records of appointments to benefices (especially the *Register of the Privy Seal*), records of Testaments and elsewhere. While gaps still remain, the evidence is adequate to show clearly enough the course of development.

It is a simple matter to draw attention to some of the considerations which, in any diocese, helped to shape the attitudes of the existing clergy to the reformation, their decision whether or not to join the reformed ministry and, consequently, at least in part, the problems confronting any bishop or superintendent as he went about his task of 'planting kirks' as the phrase ran.

One factor was the financial state of the parishes, including the stipends actually paid to the priests. In only some 14% of Scotland's parishes did all the revenues — teinds, income from land, fees and offerings — remain available in the parish to maintain an independent 'parson'. In the overwhelming majority of cases the bulk of the revenues was diverted to contribute to the maintenance of an abbey, a bishopric, a cathedral canonry or some other institution, leaving only a small balance to pay a vicar to serve in the parish. 'Appropriation' meant that the bulk of the teinds— usually the 'corn teinds', or 'teind sheaves' or 'greater teinds' — were diverted to the endowment of the appropriating institution, while for the payment of a vicar to serve the parish there remained only a slender residue, consisting sometimes of the lesser teinds — those of butter, wool, eggs, and so forth — but sometimes of a fixed annual 'pension' or 'portion' from the whole revenues of the parish. As a general rule, a monastery appointed secular priests to serve as vicars in its appropriated parishes, but houses of canons regular, like the Augustinians of Holyrood and the Premonstratensians of Whithorn and Tongland, could appoint their own monks or canons as vicars of parishes.

The initial proposal of the reformers had been to deprive all clergy of their benefices and to make no provision for their maintenance beyond that made for paupers. When this was discovered to be impracticable, the compromise already mentioned was reached whereby beneficed clergy retained their livings for life, with the exception usually of one third, and the thirds were used partly to pay stipends to the clergy of the reformed church. The latter were of four grades — first, superintendents, who were the organisers and administrators; second, ministers, who had a full commission not only to preach but to administer the sacraments; third, exhorters, who conducted services and preached but were not permitted to administer the sacraments; and, fourth, readers, who could conduct services by reading lessons, reading prayers from a service book and reading addresses from the Book of Homilies, but were not permitted to preach. These offices are not to be confused with the offices of parson, vicar, and so forth. The offices in the reformed church were differentiated by the functions which men performed; the offices of the old ecclesiastical fabric were differentiated not by function but simply by the benefices which men held. There were for a time two distinct structures, the old and the new, which coincided only in so far as some parsons and vicars happened to be at the same time ministers, exhorters or readers.

There was relatively little financial inducement to the beneficed clergy to conform to the new regime and serve as ministers, exhorters or readers. A parson or vicar was assured of two-thirds of his living for life, with no duties to perform; by undertaking service in the reformed church he merely qualified himself to retain the remaining third. Such a proposition was hardly attractive except to men who were either sincerely interested in the reformation or subjected to some manner of pressure or persuasion.

Among the regular clergy, the monks and canons regular, the position was different. The monastic ideal of community of goods and the prohibition of private property had long been lost sight of, and each monk, already before the reformation, had his individual 'portion', which he drew like a salary. The Scottish reformation did not bring with it, as is so often alleged, any 'suppression' or 'dissolution' of the monasteries. The abbot, prior, or commendator continued to administer the property of the house, the convent remained a legal corporation, and the monks still enjoyed their portions and their residential quarters. In short, all went on very much as before, except that recruitment would normally cease. A monk, therefore, had an assured income, in the shape of his 'portion', on which he could keep body and soul together. It is true that he sometimes had difficulty in securing payment of his portion;[2] but even if he drew it in full he still had somewhat greater financial inducement to serve in the reformed church than a parson or vicar had, because if a monk became a minister or a reader he received a full stipend in addition to his 'portion.'

While the pattern and proportions varied from diocese to diocese, it was in general true that many of the ministers, exhorters and readers of the reformed church were parsons and vicars who conformed and carried on their work in their parishes. It is to such men that Ninian Winzet was alluding when he wrote: 'At Pasche and certane Soundays efter, thai techeit with grete appering zele, and ministrate the sacramentis til us on the Catholik manere; and be Witsonday thai change thair standart in our plane contrare.'[3] But he also points to the numbers of monks who entered the ranks of the reformed church: 'Quhy admit ye to be your prechouris ... [men] of na experience, nor yit haifand praeeminence by utheris of godly leving, except ye call that godly to covet a fair wyfe and ane fatt pensioune, by [i.e., contrary to] the lawis of the monastik lyfe, quhilk sindry of thame hes professit.'[4] Another observer, the Jesuit de Gouda, also speaks of the monks who had turned ministers, but remarks as well on the acceptance of men with no previous clerical experience: 'The ministers, as they call them, are either apostate monks, or laymen of low rank, and are quite unlearned, being tailors, shoemakers, tanners or the like.'[5]

It was a serious problem to find sufficient men qualified to serve as ministers, and it is not surprising that there had to be so many exhorters and readers for a number of years after 1560.

It cannot be disputed that the reforming bishops played much the same rôle in 'planting kirks' as superintendents and commissioners did elsewhere: the pattern of the expansion of the reformed ministry was almost identical in their dioceses to what it was in most other areas, and when the operations of the bishops came to an end and their functions passed to 'commissioners' appointed by the general assembly there was no spectacular change for the better.[6] It seems, too, that Galloway and Orkney were more successful than any other overseers in prevailing on existing priests to continue their ministrations under the new regime.[7] It cannot, however, be claimed that the bishops were an unqualified success, any more than superintendents were: both groups were repeatedly censured by the general assembly for inefficiency of one kind or another, and superintendents frequently asked to be released from what they must have thought an unrewarding task.[8] There were obvious difficulties for all of them — shortage of funds to pay stipends, shortage of qualified men, obstacles put in their way by individuals who either opposed the reformation or were more concerned for their own financial gain than for the preaching of the gospel — difficulties for which the assembly was never prepared to make allowance. It is difficult to avoid the conclusion that there were personal animosities and very possibly there was some jealousy of superintendents who perhaps looked a little more like bishops than the compilers of the Book of Discipline had envisaged: a superintendent was entitled to a princely salary, he was styled 'lord' or 'venerable father', a countess might address him as 'Father', and on his visitations he received hospitality like other 'great men' or 'great lords' on a scale which his hosts found burdensome.[9]

1   *BUK*, i, 27
2   In 1565 two monks of Glenluce, Richard Brown and Robert Galbraith, who had been members of the community for twenty and twenty-six years respectively, raised actions against the commendator for their portions, which had been unpaid since 1559. In each case the portion consisted of eight bolls of meal and eight bolls of bere, two stones of butter and two stones of cheese, thirty loads of peats, their chambers and yards in the abbey, and £20 in money. The values are given, with slight variations between the two cases, and show that a portion was worth about £60 in the Scots money of the time — equivalent in purchasing power to perhaps £3000 sterling a year to-day — *plus* accommodation (A and D, xxxiv, 141, 352). Michael Cousin, a canon of Tongland, sued in the same year, stating that he had been a

member of the community for five years before the reformation. His portion was somewhat smaller than those of the Glenluce monks, but even so would be worth between £40 and £50 in the Scots money of the time (*ibid*, xxxiv, 114).

3   Works (STS), i, 53
4   ibid., 101
5   *Papal Negotiations with Queen Mary* (SHS), 135
6   Donaldson, *Scottish Reformation*, 87-8
7   Donaldson, *Scottish Church History*, 79
8   Donaldson, *Scottish Reformation*, 175
9   Ibid., 125-8

ALEXANDER GORDON, BISHOP OF GALLOWAY

Alexander Gordon, grandson of the third earl of Huntly, was the son of John, Lord Gordon, and of Margaret Stewart, natural daughter of King James IV by Margaret Drummond. He was thus brother of the fourth earl of Huntly and cousin of Mary, Queen of Scots; through his maternal grandmother and by his mother's second marriage he was connected with the powerful Perthshire family of Drummond. Born about 1516, he spent much of his youth in the company of his uncle, James V, who was some four years his senior. We know nothing of his education, but from his style of 'Master' we may assume that he graduated Master of Arts.

The story of Gordon's life from 1544 to 1560 is a tale of successive attempts to establish him in one of the Scottish bishoprics[1]. The greater benefices were at that time almost the preserve of noble families and a vacancy often led to a struggle, in which victory went to the house possessing most influence with the government. During the minority of Queen Mary, the Huntly family was attached to the party of the Queen Mother, Mary of Guise, in her contest for power with the earl of Arran, governor of Scotland. In 1544 the triumph of the Dowager, with Cardinal Beaton, bore fruit in rewards for her supporters, and Alexander Gordon was nominated and elected to the bishopric of Caithness. A four years' struggle ensued with Robert Stewart, administrator of that see, who was ultimately allowed to retain the bishopric. The Dowager next made an attempt to place Gordon in Glasgow, but was unable to overcome the opposition of Arran (still governor) to his candidature. Gordon, who, in expectation of his preferment, had gone to Rome in 1550 and had been consecrated there, was solaced by the titular dignity of archbishop of Athens and the more substantial commendatorship of Inchaffray (1551). In 1553 he was provided to the Isles, with Iona *in commendam*. The completion of his title to these benefices was somehow prevented, possibly through the fall of the Huntly family from favour in 1554, when Mary of Guise, now governor, began to pursue an intensely French policy which alienated much Scottish sympathy. From some years Alexander Gordon was styled archbishop of Athens, postulate or elect of the Isles, commendator of Inchaffray and Iona.

The see of Galloway became vacant in September, 1558, by the death of Andrew Durie, who, according to Knox,[2] died of shock after a protestant riot in Edinburgh. The Huntly family was once more in favour, and the earl had become lieutenant-general of the kingdom. Alexander Gordon was nominated to Galloway early in 1559.[3] Some defect in his title long persisted. The appointment never received papal confirmation (which was legally necessary until the pope's authority in Scotland was abrogated in August 1560); and the crown from time to time acted as if the bishopric was vacant — the temporality was gifted to the earl of Eglinton in January 1560, and pensions were granted in July 1561 and June 1563.[4] Possibly the explanation of the crown's action might be found in the relations of the house of Huntly with successive governments: for instance, the gift to Eglinton may have been due to signs that Alexander Gordon and his uncle Huntly were inclining towards support for the protestant revolt. However, it is clear that, while Gordon remained technically 'bishop elect', he was for all practical purposes bishop from 1559 or 1560. In September 1560, a month after the 'Reformation Parliament', he wrote to the English ambassador requesting a 'passport general' for the people of his diocese — his 'diocesianis'[5] — in terms which suggest that he was not aware that anything had changed. And he had effective possession of the revenues of the see from 1561 at latest.

The value of the see, with the annexed abbey of Tongland, is given in contemporary records. The annual income in cash is stated variously as £1226 14s and £1137 6s 8d. There were in addition quantities of bere (8 chalders, 7 bolls or 6 chalders, 15 bolls, 3 pecks), of meal (10 c. 7 b. or 7 c. 9 b.), of malt (8 b.), and of salmon (268). These rents were worth an additional £200 or so in 1561 and their money equivalent increased as prices rose in succeeding years. The total revenue may be put at about £1400. The abbey of Inchaffray, set in tack to the Drummonds, yielded £666 13s 4d yearly. The impressive total of Gordon's income — over £2000 Scots — was, however, subject to the deduction of a number of pensions. The fact is that the 'tulchan' principle, which received its quaint name in the 1570s, was already notorious in the previous generation, when episcopal appointments were almost invariably accompanied by grants of pensions, often on such a scale that the fruits were in substance divided among laymen, leaving to the bishop only a modest competence. In this instance, Sir John Maxwell of Terregles had a pension variously stated to be £500, 600 merks or 500 merks, and he undoubtedly received £500 in 1561 and 1562; Thomas Stewart, son of the laird of Garlies, had a grant from the crown on 18 January 1563 of a pension of 100 merks; on 18 July 1561 Stephen Wilson was granted one of £150; on 2 March 1564 Archibald Crawford, parson of Eaglesham, received a crown gift, with the bishop's consent, of a pension of 600 merks; and the bishop himself granted some smaller pensions. Those pensions are together approximately equal to the *money* revenues of the bishopric; there may have been others besides those mentioned, and no doubt Inchaffray also was burdened with pensions. How many of the pensions from the bishopric were being paid concurrently is not clear; moreover, we know that Stephen Wilson's pension was not paid, at least before 1568, and there was litigation about Archibald Crawford's. The whole position remains obscure, but so far as one can see the bishop's net income cannot have been greatly in excess of the

£500 to £700 which was regarded as a comfortable salary for an ecclesiastical administrator of the period[6]. (When this article was originally written, in 1947, we thought of a multiplier of about 15 to give some indication of the equivalent of the sterling of 1560, and as the £ Scots of 1560 was worth about 1/5 of sterling, this meant in practice multiplying by 3; after another forty years of an inflation not paralleled in the last four centuries we require multiplication by at least another 15, so that Gordon's £700 would be worth not £2000 as in 1947 but over £30,000 today — and far more if the incidence of taxation is taken into account.)

Alexander Gordon's career down to 1560 had been a search for a settled and eminent position in the church. Self-interest had no doubt been the main motive, and that motive continued to exert a strong influence on his life in succeeding years. We should not, however, forget that in the 1540s he had shown a very strong loyalty to the Queen Mother even when her cause was not in the ascendant, and we shall see that he later exhibited a similar enthusiasm in his attachment to her daughter, Queen Mary. There is little in what we know of his life which gives any clue as to his probable attitude to the religious revolt of 1559-60. But two points should be noted: possibly, like his brother the earl, he had been alienated from the conservative cause in the late 1550s by the Dowager's disregard of Scottish national sentiment; and it seems that, generally speaking, those bishops who were well entrenched in their benefices tended to be more orthodox than those who, like Gordon, were less firmly established.

Whatever his motives and whatever his opinions, Gordon's actions left no doubt of his attachment to the reformed cause even while the issue of the protestant revolt was still in doubt. He was later to claim that he had been 'the first that publicly preached Christ Jesus in face of the authority (that is, in defiance of the government)'.[7] In September 1559 he was associated with the protestant lords, and in the following month he was, along with Knox, Goodman, and Willock, a member of their council for religion. With Knox he long continued to be on peculiarly intimate terms. In the early months of 1560 he was in the reformers' inmost councils and seems to have influenced his brother, Huntly, who was not a strong party man, towards the reformed side. Of the four bishops present at the reformation parliament in August 1560, Gordon was the only one committed to the cause of reform; he was described as having 'renounced papistry and openly professed Jesus Christ' with the reformers. Knox, three years later, expressed his conviction that the bishop's conversion had been quite genuine. Shortly after the parliament we find him preaching earnestly—when preachers were few—and praying heartily for Queen Elizabeth (on whom, in certain circumstances, the maintenance of the work of reformation might depend). In January 1561 Gordon signed the Book of Discipline, the reformers' scheme of church polity.[8]

The reformation made it possible for the bishop to acknowledge his wife.[9] The lady was Barbara Logie, apparently a daughter of David Logie of King's Cramond and a sister of Robert Logie. The bishop and she had been married in all but name for some seventeen years, and had a family, including John, born about 1544, in whose favour his father made a resignation of his bishopric in 1568 and who later became dean of Salisbury; George, who had a gift of the bishopric of Galloway in 1586; Laurence, who had the temporality of the bishopric for a time and became commendator of Glenluce; Robert; Alexander; William; and Barbara, who married Anthony Stewart, parson of Penningham, a son of Alexander Stewart of Garlies. Professional rules alone had hitherto debarred Gordon from formal matrimony; but references to his children, born before 1560 out of lawful wedlock, continue for some time to be decently reticent about their relationship to the bishop.

Gordon's support for the reformation was clearly enough defined. How a place could be found for such a prelate in the reformed church was explained in general in the Introduction, but at what date Gordon began to act as an overseer, carrying out the functions of a superintendent, is uncertain. There is until 1563 no record of any legislation by a general assembly commissioning him to act; there may never have been such legislation, but the early registers of the assemblies are very defective. The evidence for the beginning of his work is to be found in financial records — the Accounts of the Collectors of Thirds of Benefices. For the year 1561 the third of the bishopric of Galloway was duly received by the collector-general, and this should indicate that Gordon was not at that time acting in the reformed church. On the other hand, as the bishop had never been forbidden to exercise his episcopal functions his diocesans would still expect him to act as bishop; moreover, in 1561 there were already some ministers and readers at work in the diocese, and, so far as we know, no official other than the bishop had authority to admit them to their offices.[10] In 1562 Gordon's position is clear beyond doubt. He was now officially recognised as 'overseer' of his diocese, classed among the reformed clergy and, in common with all beneficed men who served in the reformed church, allowed to retain the third of his revenues which would otherwise have been uplifted by the collector general. Exactly the same was done in the following year, when the bishop was styled 'Mr Alexander Gordon, superintendent of Galloway.'[11]

The position thus achieved was satisfactory neither to the bishop nor to the general assembly. In June 1562 the bishop asked for formal appointment as a superintendent; such an appointment would extend the scope of his labours to Carrick and Dumfriesshire, but would entitle him to a superintendent's salary in addition to his third. The request was refused by the assembly.[12] The assembly of December 1562, however, consented to put the names of Gordon and Robert Pont, minister of Dunkeld, in a leet for election to the superintendentship of Galloway, the election to take place in April; as an interim measure, Gordon was given a commission to 'admit ministers, exhorters and readers and to do such other things as were before accustomed in planting of kirks.'[13] For some reason the proposed election was never held. John Knox, in his *History*, takes credit to himself for having discovered a plan of Gordon to bribe the electors, but his narrative is a curiously confused one in which Knox describes himself as also defending the bishop's character when Queen Mary said: 'If you knew him [Gordon] as well as I do, you would never promote him to that office, nor yet to any other within your kirk ... That man is a dangerous man'. According to his own account, Knox retorted that 'if he [Gordon] fear not God now, he deceives many more than me', and added that Gordon was 'at that time the man that was most familiar with the said John, in his house and at table'.[14] The real reason why no election took place may well have been the reason which, as explained in the Introduction, always militated against the election of more superintendents, namely the lack of funds to pay their rather lavish salaries. We may not be far wrong if we conclude that, while Gordon demanded appointment as superintendent with the appropriate salary, the assembly insisted that he should act without formal appointment and be content with the remission of his third.[15] At any rate, after the frustration of the April election, the assembly of June 1563 renewed its commission to Galloway, along with Orkney and Caithness, to 'plant kirks,' etc., in 'his bounds,' which were simply those of his diocese, Nithsdale being expressly allotted to the superintendent of Glasgow.[16]

From 1562 until 1568 Gordon was known as 'commissioner,' 'overseer,' or 'superintendent' of Galloway, and was frequently present at general assemblies in that capacity.[17] His duties were, briefly, the organising of congregations, the admission of clergy, the inspection of parochial work, disciplinary action against erring clergy, the imposition of penance on moral offenders, and the giving of judgment in matrimonial cases. The evidence that Gordon did perform those functions is substantial. In the first place, the remission of his third in consideration of his labours as an overseer, already mentioned for 1562 and 1563, was approved by the general assembly in 1563[18] and evidently continued year by year. The accounts for Galloway are not indeed extant for 1564-7, but a note in the 1571 account makes it clear that the bishop had enjoyed the allowance in 1567, and the 1568 account shows him still enjoying his remission as 'overseer'.[19] There can be no doubt that the remission was continuous from 1562 to 1568. In view of the poverty of the reformed church in those years, it is inconceivable that good money was paid to a man doing nothing to earn it.

It is only casual references which provide evidence of Gordon's presence in his diocese in those years, but we do know that he was at Tongland in April and June, 1564; May, 1566; and (probably) January, 1567.[20] No doubt a further examination of charters would yield additional evidence. A good deal of the administration could, however, be conducted by writing or by deputies while the bishop was in Edinburgh, at Stirling, or at his abbey of Inchaffray. We know from one casual reference that he was regarded as the proper judge in matrimonial causes, for in June 1563 the laird of Garlies, younger, complained that the bishop had not done justice to Margaret Murray when she raised an action against her husband, Godfrey MacCulloch, for non-adherence. Six months later we find the bishop, along with the superintendent of Fife, delating four women to the general assembly for witchcraft.[21] There was one notable occasion when Gordon exercised his ministerial functions outside his diocese — he officiated at the marriage of Jane Gordon, his niece, to James Hepburn, earl of Bothwell. One of the witnesses at the subsequent divorce proceedings described this ceremony as having taken place 'before Fastern's Eve [Shrove Tuesday] was a year' — one of many indications that the observance of Lent did not die out as quickly as some of the reformers desired. The date was actually 24 February 1565/6, which was Quinquagesima Sunday. A contemporary account of the marriage stressed that the bishop preached, 'which of long time has been rare among us.'[22] Bishop Gordon was, of course, entitled to give collation to benefices in his diocese and to provide to those which were at his own presentation. When the vicarage of Sorbie fell vacant by the death of Gilbert Oislar, Gordon provided Robert Blindsheill, minister of Wigtown, in June 1566. In the following November he filled the vicarage of Whithorn by appointing John Kay, an ex-monk whose name does not appear among the reformed clergy[23]. General assemblies did not hesitate to make use of the bishop's abilities. In December 1566 he was appointed a member of a committee to modify an answer which William Ramsay, a master of St. Salvator's College, had prepared to a book written by Bullinger, the famous Swiss divine, on the delicate question of the enforcement of the use of vestments in the Church of England.[24] After July 1567, when the collection and distribution of the thirds of benefices became a task for superintendents and commissioners, Gordon took action in the financial administration of his diocese.[25]

The chief significance of Gordon's career in the context of the progress of the reformation lies in his dealings with the clergy of the diocese and the extent to which the ministry of the reformed church was spread throughout the bounds of his jurisdiction. What has to be studied, in short, is the organisation of the diocese and the manner in which the bishop operated within it.

At the period of the reformation, the diocese of Galloway contained forty-five parishes, being all the parishes of Wigtown and those of Kirkcudbright west of the Urr[26] (while the remainder of Kirkcudbright, with Dumfriesshire, formed part of the diocese of Glasgow). Only five of the parishes — Dalry, Kirkchrist, Parton, Stoneykirk, and Wigtown[27] — were independent parsonages, all the others being 'appropriated,' chiefly to monastic houses. Whithorn Priory had thirteen of the parishes; Holyrood, five or six; Tongland, four; Sweetheart, three; Dundrennan and Soulseat each had two; Glenluce and the priory of St. Mary's Isle each had one. While most of the Galloway parishes were thus appropriated to abbeys, two were appropriated to the bishopric and one to the archdeaconry. The Chapel Royal of Stirling was endowed with five Galloway parishes. In these cases the prebendary of the Chapel who drew his revenues from a Galloway parish was known by the title of that parish, *e.g.*, 'parson of Balmaclellan'; but he was an absentee, and there was, or ought to have been, a vicar serving the parish. The proportion of appropriated parishes in Galloway was very high — 89 per cent. — but in other districts of Scotland figures ranging from 75 per cent. to 100 per cent. are to be found.

How far there may have been genuine interest in the reforming movement among the rank and file of the Galloway clergy it is hardly possible to say. There had been the celebrated case of John Mackbrair, a monk of Glenluce, who in 1550 was imprisoned for heresy and whose subsequent career as a reformer is well enough known.[28] Some of the landed families, again, lost no time in attaching themselves to the reformed cause, for Sir Alexander Stewart of Garlies and Sir John Gordon of Lochinvar were among those who signed the Book of Discipline in January 1561.[29] The district can hardly have been unaffected by the proximity of the strongly protestant areas of Ayrshire; while on the other side of the country, John, Master of Maxwell, who by marriage became Lord Herries, had an almost heroic career as one of the Lords of the Congregation. It would be unreasonable to exclude the possibility that some of the clergy may have been of the same mind as the lairds. Besides, the influence of a local laird might very well be brought to bear on a parish priest. Account must also be taken of the likelihood that the Galloway clergy were influenced by the example, the precept, and perhaps even the pressure of their bishop, who had himself embraced the reformed faith with enthusiasm.

Those absentee titulars, the prebendaries of the Chapel Royal, had no financial inducement whatever to serve in the reformed church, because the whole of their revenues, and not only two-thirds, were secured to them in respect of their functions in the chapel. None of them took part in the work of the reformed church, at least in this diocese. Of the five genuine parsons, we know that Richard Balfour (Kirkchrist) became minister in the parish, and that Neil MacDowell (Stoneykirk) became reader in his. Charles Geddes was parson of Parton, and if he be identical with the Mr Charles Geddes who was a servitor of the Master of Maxwell he must have been on the reforming side; it seems likely that he became a reader, for no other reader or exhorter is recorded in the parish between 1563 and 1570. The parson of Wigtown was Patrick Vaus, eminent as a lawyer and politician but not a serious ecclesiastic. The parson of Dalry — whether or not he was the John Hepburn who had held office in 1556 — evidently did not serve his parish after the Reformation. Thus, out of five parsons, certainly two and very likely three served in the reformed church.[30]

Interest centres, however, on the vicars. In number they must have been about forty, the number of appropriated parishes; but, on the one hand, there were a few cases where one vicar was holding a pair of vicarages in plurality, while, on the other, an independent parish, which had a parson, sometimes had a vicar as well — as an assistant, which happened in Dalry. There is no register or list of the clergy who were in office at the reformation, and the names must be collected from a variety of sources in which they occur sporadically. The names of some twenty-three of the men who held Galloway vicarages at the reformation have been obtained with complete, or well-nigh complete, certainty, and those of another thirteen with varying degrees of probability or possibility. Of those thirty-six, three held two vicarages each, so that among them they account for thirty-eight parishes.

The vicarages of Borgue and Mochrum were held respectively by James Scott and John Stevenson, each a lord of session and a pluralist with his interests and career lying quite outwith the church. The vicarages of Inch and Leswalt belonged to sir William MacDowell, a pluralist, who held also the vicarages of Dalmeny and Holyroodhouse and one or two chaplainries; he was Master of Works to the queen, and, although his name suggests a local origin, he was clearly a careerist not likely to serve in a Galloway parish. Gilbert Ostler, vicar of Sorbie, was another pluralist, who held chaplainries in Perth and Dundee. Balmaghie and Kirkcudbright seem to have been held in plurality by George Crichton, a canon of Holyrood, the house to which those parishes were appropriated. His interests clearly lay elsewhere; and indeed none of the parishes appropriated to that distant abbey can show a vicar who served his cure in Galloway under the reformed regime. John Martin, a canon of Whithorn, also held a pair of vicarages in plurality — Gelston and Longcastle. Among all the pluralist vicars, Martin is the only one who possibly served in the reformed church, and even in his case it seems unlikely. This might suggest that, while the holder of a single vicarage was induced by the prospect of retaining his third, the more comfortably-off pluralist was not so tempted; yet this can hardly be pressed, for even with two vicarages a man might still have a very small income, while it may be that the pluralists were necessarily of a less conscientious type and so less likely to be moved by religious motives. One another case should be mentioned here — that of Kirkcormock, which had been held since so long ago as 1521 by sir Herbert Dun, who was by 1560 'ane auld blind man' whose days of useful work were over. But, while he could not himself take part in the work of the reformed church, this old priest did the next best thing by sending his sons. He had two sons — Michael, who succeeded his father in his vicarage and became an exhorter, and Cuthbert, who became a reader. The vicars so far mentioned were all men who had quite intelligible motives for not appearing among the reformed clergy; at least there are reasons which explain their absence from those ranks. There was, indeed, only one vicar who clearly did not serve in the reformed church and for whom neither explanation nor excuse can be offered — Robert Watson (Clayshant).

On the other hand, there were nine vicars who seem to have embraced the reformation with enthusiasm, and almost at once became readers or exhorters:

Martin Gib (Penninghame), John Johnston (Whithorn), Patrick MacCulloch (Wigtown), Donald Muir (Kells), John Parker (Buittle), Ralph Peirson (Kirkmaiden in Farines), John Sanderson (Glenluce), John Stewart (Minnigaff), and William Telfer (Cruggleton). It is true that Gib and Peirson are first recorded as in the service of the reformed church in 1561, Telfer in 1562, Johnston, Parker, Sanderson, Stewart, and MacCulloch in 1563, and Muir not until 1567; but in the light of the information at our disposal it would not be safe to conclude that they were converted to the reformed faith at different dates. Nor should we exaggerate the depth of their conversion. There were those who conformed to what seemed for the time to be the fashion, the prevailing opinion, but were equally ready to change again. For instance, William Telfer, who was vicar of Cruggleton, appears as a reader in 1562 and so continues for twenty years. Yet in 1563 we find that a sir William Telfer was convicted for saying mass at a place rendered by Pitcairn as 'Congiltoun'; but this is a mis-reading for 'Crugiltoun,' and it appears that the vicar-reader was quite prepared to do a little mass-mongering when the mass was in fashion. We may associate with those vicars who thus served in the reformed church William Vaus, who had been curate at Longcastle in 1556 and became reader there by 1568; he later succeeded John Martin in the vicarage.

Michael Hawthorn, a priest of the diocese since 1549 and vicar of Toskerton since March 1559/60, and Malcolm MacCulloch, vicar of Anwoth from 1558, made their first appearances as readers only in 1572; and John White, a monk — perhaps of Soulseat — and vicar of Kirkmaiden in Rhinns, does not appear as a reader until 1574. By those dates — 1572 and 1574 — the triumph of the reforming party was secure and the prospect of any counter-reformation was very dim. It may be, therefore, that Hawthorn, MacCulloch, and White had deferred committing themselves to the reformed church until it was clear that it had prevailed. They may, equally, have been moved by fear of deprivation; it was proposed in 1572 and passed into law in the following year that clergy who would not accept the reformed Confession of Faith should be deprived,[31] and this measure must have had a stimulating effect on waverers.

There are four more cases of vicars who served their cures in the reformed church, but it is not quite certain whether they had been in office at the reformation. Robert Muir, certainly a priest, was exhorter or reader at Girthon from 1563; he is not styled vicar until 1574, but he may have held the vicarage by 1560. Thomas Regnall, a priest, was vicar and reader of Kirkdale in 1567; it seems likely that he had been vicar at the reformation. William Sharpro, a canon of Tongland, was reader at Tongland by 1563, and, although not styled vicar until 1568, had very probably held the vicarage earlier. James Thomson was reader at Soulseat by 1563; we learn only twenty years later, after his death, that he had been a canon of Soulseat and vicar of that parish, but it seems likely that he had been in office at the reformation.

Besides those vicars who served in their own parishes, there were others who served in the reformed church, but at other parishes in the district — sir Herbert Anderson, vicar of Kelton by 1549, appears as reader at Troqueer in 1579; and Mr Robert Blindshiel, who may have been vicar of Kirkandrews at the reformation, became minister at Wigtown. It is not impossible that the John MacClellan who was reader at Sennik in 1563 and at Kirkandrews from 1567 to 1586 was the John (or James) MacClellan who was vicar of Dunrod in 1561. There is also the case of John Row, who seems to have succeeded another pluralist, James Moutray, in the vicarages of Twynholm and Terregles about 1560. He was the well-known minister of Perth. Curiously enough, he did make an appearance in Galloway, when he was appointed commissioner for the district after the general assembly withdrew its approval from Bishop Alexander Gordon, but it is hardly likely that he was chosen for this task because he happened to hold two local vicarages: indeed, these benefices must have been an embarrassment to him if he attempted to deal with pluralist and non-resident clergy.

Andrew Davidson, vicar of Sennick, is something of a man of mystery, who defies classification. He was already a claimant to this vicarage in 1555; he subsequently acquired the parsonage of Kinnettles and the vicarage of Dalkeith, and when these benefices were confirmed to him in 1566 he was styled 'preacher'. On the other hand, he seems to have been in favour with John Hamilton, archbishop of St. Andrews and commendator of Paisley, who was no friend to the Knoxian reformation, and Davidson seems actually to have been on trial for saying mass at Paisley in 1563; nor does his name appear as a minister, exhorter or reader. He retained his three benefices until his death in or about 1587.

In seven cases, although the name is recorded of a vicar shortly before or shortly after 1560, it is impossible to say whether or not he held office at that critical date — Thomas Acoltrane (Kirkmadrine), William Brown (Kirkinner or Kirkcowan), Adam Cutler (Rerrick), David Forman (Dalry), James MacAllan (Kirkcolm), John Martin (Crossmichael), and Robert Stewart (Glasserton). At any rate, in none of these parishes did the vicar serve in the ministry of the reformed church. There are, further, two parishes to which a vicar cannot be assigned even conjecturally — Balmaclellan and Kirkmabreck.

Summing up the evidence, it appears that twelve vicars served in the reformed church in their own parishes, four more probably did likewise, while a further three seem to have served in other parishes: that is, nineteen out of about thirty-six: and of those thirty-six, it will be recalled, about half a dozen had understandable reasons for not appearing among the reformed clergy. While the figures are incomplete and tentative, they do indicate a quite remarkable readiness on the part of the Galloway vicars to continue the care of their flocks under the new regime.

The canons regular of Whithorn and Tongland — who, of course, had the tradition of serving parish churches as vicars — show a similar record of service in the reformed church. Both were peculiarly subject to the influence of the bishop, because the canons of Whithorn were the chapter of the bishopric, and the bishop was commendator of Tongland. In Whithorn there was, indeed, the contrary influence of the prior, Malcolm Fleming, who was a rigid conservative and a strong opponent of the reformation, but his views evidently did not command much following among his monks. There were twelve canons at Whithorn in 1560, but one of them — Frederick Bruce, the subprior — disappears from the scene after the beginning of that year, and must be presumed to have died shortly afterwards. Out of the eleven who survived the reformation, two — William Cranston and John Poltavie or Pogawe — clearly did not take part in the work of the reformed church, although they survived for another twenty years, or more; but of the others, Adam Fleming, John Johnston, John Kay, Ralph Peirson, George Stevenson, John Stewart, and William Telfer certainly became readers, George Muir probably did so and John Martin may have done so. Thus, out of eleven canons of Whithorn, certainly seven and perhaps as many as nine served in the reformed church. In the case of Tongland, we have the names of eight canons who survived the reformation — or nine if we include Ralph Peirson, the subprior, who was also a canon of Whithorn. Three of them — John Matheson, Michael Cousin, and Edward Hering — took no part in the work of the reformed church, but the others —Patrick Grant, James MacCulloch, Thomas MacUthre or MacCutrie, James Mair, William Sharpro, and, of course, Peirson — appear as readers. It is noteworthy that with hardly an exception the churches in which the canons of Whithorn and Tongland served as readers or exhorters were churches which had been annexed to their houses before the reformation; appropriations, which had been one of the evils of the unreformed church, in this way worked to the advantage of the church reformed.

Of the monks of Dundrennan,[32] the only one who may have entered the service of the reformed church was John Wright, for there was a reader of that name at Gelston in 1563. In the case of Glenluce, we have the names of no less than fifteen monks who were alive in 1560,[33] and of those fifteen monks not one appears as a minister, exhorter, or reader in the diocese of Galloway. The sharp contrast between Whithorn and Tongland on the one hand and Dundrennan and Glenluce on the other would suggest that monks were turned into ministers or readers not by financial pressure — which operated everywhere alike; nor yet by conscience — which might be presumed to operate everywhere in the same proportion; but by leadership or by influence, which was present at Whithorn and Tongland but not at Dundrennan or Glenluce. Little is known of the attitudes of the abbots of those houses, but the indications are that they were not sympathetic to the reformation.

The year 1563 is the first for which we have full details of the staff of the reformed church. There were by that time in Galloway seven or eight ministers, six exhorters, and twenty-five readers—a total of nearly forty reformed clergy for the forty-five parishes of the diocese, which represents a very considerable effort in a short space of time. In 1567 the total was still very much the same, and by 1574 it had risen to only about fifty. Clearly, viewed in relation to the rather meagre expansion between 1563 and 1574, the achievement of the first three years looks even more remarkable. And one can go further. While 1563 is the first year for which we have full details, there are figures for the total sums paid in stipends in the two preceding years, and these give some indication of the general picture. The figures available are for a very large area — not only Wigtown, Kirkcudbright, Dumfries, and Annandale, but also Stirling, Lanark, Renfrew, and Dumbarton — and they are £2700 in 1561 and £3174 in 1562. Then in 1563, when that vast district was divided, the four southern counties have a total of £1566, the remainder one of £1831, and the over-all figure is thus £3397 — that is, only £200 more than in 1562 and £700 more than in 1561. Since we know what the 1563 figure meant in terms of personnel, we can argue back. Assuming — and it is a reasonable assumption — that the increase had been spread evenly over all the counties, we can conclude that the staff of the reformed church in Galloway was only some 6 or 7 per cent. less in 1562 than in 1563, and that even in 1561, the first year of the reformed church, it was only some 20 per cent. less than in 1563. In other words, we must visualise some thirty ministers, exhorters, and readers already at work in the diocese of Galloway in 1561.

Out of the seven or eight ministers who were installed in Galloway by 1563, only two were certainly local men — Richard Balfour at Kirkchrist and Robert Blindshiel at Wigtown. John Gibson, minister of Stoneykirk, Toskerton, and Clayshant, may have been a Dominican friar of Wigtown and James Dodds, minister at Dalry, had quite possibly been prior of that friary. John McGhie, minister at Kirkcowan, has a name which suggests a local origin, but nothing whatever is known of him. On the other hand, Adam Fowlis, at Whithorn, was imported, for he had been vicar of Tealing, in Angus, and a prebendary of the collegiate church of St. Mary in St. Andrews; and William Moscrop, who in 1563 had charge of Anwoth, Girthon, St. Mary's Isle, Kirkandrews, Borgue, and Sennick, is probably to be identified with the monk of Jedburgh who bore that somewhat rare name. Of Alexander Allardyce, at Kirkcudbright, we know nothing, but had he been a local man some evidence would probably have emerged. The fact that the Galloway clergy produced so few ministers would suggest that their quality was not very high; those of them who went over to the reformed church were for the most part fit to be only exhorters or readers.

Among the exhorters of 1563, we find that Cuthbert Adair (Inch) had been a chaplain at Whithorn in 1557, and Michael Dun (Kirkcudbright) had been a priest of the diocese since 1550. John Sanderson (Glenluce) and John Stewart (Minnigaff) were the vicars of those parishes. The name of John Crawford, exhorter at Penninghame, is that of a chaplain recorded in 1558. Alexander

Hunter (Kirkcolm) and John Dury (Parton) have not been identified. That is, out of six exhorters, four or five were local clergy.

Of the readers, perhaps as many as nine were pre-reformation parish clergy serving their parishes, and have already been mentioned. Two were priests, but unbeneficed — Robert Champan (Balmaghie) and John Moffat (Kirkchrist). John Dunbar, reader in Kirkmadrine, may be identical with a chaplain of that name. Eight or nine were monks, already mentioned, four of them being also numbered among the beneficed clergy. Of Francis Home (Dalry) it has emerged only that he had been associated with Bishop Gordon in 1559. There are, therefore, six or seven of the readers of 1563 who remain unidentified — Thomas MacAlexander (Leswalt), John MacCaill (Sorbie), Donald MacAllan (Kirkandrews), Elias MacCulloch (Balmacclellan), one Thomson, Christian name unknown (Clayshant), and James Wylie (Anwoth). It seems rather unlikely that Henry Smith, at Glasserton, had been the Ayr friar of that name. Five of them, from their surnames, were obviously local men. But collectively they may represent the tailors, shoemakers, tanners, and the like of whom de Gouda wrote contemptuously. Yet the proportion — about three-fifths — of the Galloway readers who had previously been priests or monks is sufficiently impressive.

As already mentioned, some more of the local clergy made their appearance in the ranks of the ministers and readers at later dates, after 1563, but as the years went on the proportion of reformed clergy drawn from this source was bound to diminish, and analyses for, say, 1567 and 1572 might be misleading. The figures for 1563 amply demonstrate that continuity in personnel was a conspicuous feature of the reformation in Galloway.

A key question is the attribution of responsibility for the rapidity with which the 'planting' of ministers, readers and exhorters went ahead in the diocese of Galloway. Who was responsible for examining the qualifications of these clergy, for admitting them to their charges, for bringing about the increase in their numbers between 1561 and 1567, for supervising their work, and, in short, for the whole organisation of what seems to have been a fairly thriving church in the diocese? There were no presbyteries, there was no synod except one which the bishop might summon twice in a year, there were not, so far as we know, other commissioners empowered to work in Galloway. The work must have been that of Alexander Gordon. A similar argument, applied to the consistorial jurisdiction, points to the bishop as judge in matrimonial and possibly testamentary cases between 1560 and the appointment of commissaries by the government in 1564.

Yet the success which the bishop apparently had initially, and the acceptability of his labours, were evidently not maintained. The reason is to be found in some of the other activities which helped to shape his life. His abbey of Inchaffray occupied a good deal of his attention in the earlier 1560s, but before the middle of 1565 he had resigned it in favour of one of his cousins, the

Drummonds (pensions being reserved to his sons, John and Laurence).[34] As bishop of Galloway, Gordon was dean of the chapel royal of Stirling, which had been annexed to the bishopric by Pope Julius II. in 1504. His duties in that capacity sometimes put him in a curious position, for the queen was using the chapel royal largely to maintain her chaplains, who, according to the statute of 1560, were 'mass-mongers' liable to heavy penalties; and yet were obliged to apply to the protestant bishop for institution in their dignities.[35] Whether by way of his position in the chapel royal or not, Gordon became increasingly an adherent of the court and of the queen, who may have thought it worth her while to use her charms to attach to herself one whom she had considered 'a dangerous man'. On 5 November 1565 Alexander Gordon took his oath as a privy councillor, and on 26 November he was admitted a senator of the college of justice; until the end of Mary's reign he was in quite regular attendance as a judge.[36] The Huntly family had been out of favour since the rebellion of the 4th earl in 1562, but they were now rehabilitated; the bishop used his influence on behalf of his nephew, the 5th earl, and the family was in favour with the queen until the close of her reign. As a courtier, the bishop did not lose sight of the interests of the reformed church, and even his enemies acknowledged that he used his influence with the queen to secure an improvement in its financial position. He obtained not only 'a good answer and fair promises' in the matter of the assignation of thirds to ministers, but also a gift by the queen to the ministers of a temporary supplement to their stipends, in December 1566.[37] In the critical months which preceded and followed the Darnley murder the queen showed a marked readiness to come to terms with the reformed church; Alexander Gordon's cordial relations with her are simply one symptom of this trend, though it must never be forgotten that she was his cousin.

In successive general assemblies there was criticism of the bishop. The young laird of Garlies brought two complaints — neither of them very serious — against him in 1563.[38] In December 1564 it was implied that he had not taken adequate care to examine the qualification of the men whom he had admitted as ministers, exhorters, and readers.[39] A year later, in an assembly which made a general condemnation of pastors who did not reside among their flocks, Gordon was accused of neglecting his duties and 'excused himself with the building of his nephew's house'.[40] In December 1567 it was stated that 'Alexander, called bishop of Galloway, commissioner, ... had not visited these three years bygone the kirks within his charge; that he .... haunted court too much, and had now purchased to be one of the session and privy council, which cannot agree with the office of a pastor or bishop.'[41] In the new ecclesiastical situation, the ministers seem to have taken special pleasure in criticising dignitaries, and the charges against superintendents, from time to time, were quite as serious as those against bishops. Yet, in conjunction with our knowledge of Gordon's growing preoccupation with worldly affairs, these complaints indicate that his enthusiasm for the labours of a superintendent had evaporated. Possibly he never gave willing service after the assembly's refusal to pay him a salary. In addition, he may have shared a prevalent disappointment as the fair prospects of establishment and endowment entertained in 1560 became more and more remote; there was poverty, perhaps starvation, among the reformed clergy, and other superintendents frequently asked to be relieved of their burdensome and sometimes ill-paid duties.

The friendship of the Gordons with the earl of Bothwell survived his divorce from Lady Jane Gordon and his marriage with Queen Mary; Alexander was a witness to the marriage contract.[42] After Mary's fall, the memory of the Corrichie campaign of 1562, when the earl of Moray had been responsible for the rout and death of Huntly, made collaboration with Moray as regent impossible. The bishop was by this time primarily a courtier; but apart from family interest his opinions as a royalist in politics and a moderate in religion would have led him to support the queen's party against the regent, who was at once an usurper and the idol of the more extreme party in the kirk. The Marian party included not only Hamiltons and Gordons who had their family quarrels with Moray, and not only papalists who recognised the restoration of Mary as their one hope, but a number of moderate protestants and non-Roman catholics; men of the centre who, perhaps less zealous and certainly less vocal than the extremists, have never received the attention they deserve. For a time, indeed, both the bishop and his nephew the earl temporized; they attended Moray's parliament in 1567 and the bishop remained in Edinburgh in the following months.[43] But from the summer of 1568 onwards they were convinced and open Marians.

The assembly of December 1567 had shown itself sufficiently hostile to Alexander, on purely ecclesiastical grounds, even when his attitude to the new government was benevolent. He had, indeed, received a fresh commission, with admonition to be diligent in visitation,[44] but he could clearly expect no mercy after he committed himself wholly to the queen's cause. The assembly of July 1568 delivered an ultimatum: the commissioner of Galloway must come to Edinburgh at the time of the next parliament to show his diligence in the charge committed to him and to answer whether he would await on court and council or upon preaching the word and planting kirks. John Row was appointed to visit Galloway.[45] Presentations were no longer directed to the bishop, and he was forbidden to take up his thirds.[46] The assembly, however, had no executive power and the government which maintained it controlled only part of the country. It is not surprising, therefore, to find that the assembly of July 1569 found it necessary to renew its prohibition of Gordon's exercise of spiritual functions and of his uplifting his thirds. An action was raised against him and the bishop was 'put to the horn' for non-payment of thirds, but by 1572 the kirk had not succeeded in making him disgorge the thirds for 1569 and later years, and he remained 'at the horn'.[47]

Gordon was prominent among the Marians as long as the civil war lasted. He remained in possession of his revenues, he continued to exercise spiritual functions as a minister. He once occupied the pulpit of the church of St Giles in Edinburgh, whence John Knox had fled when the Queen's men occupied the town, and the substance of his sermon, on 17 June 1571, is reported. Speaking in the presence of the leaders of the Queen's Party, he preached on 'charity' and argued that Mary's moral delinquencies did not disqualify her as a ruler: 'Sanct David was a sinner, and so is she; Sanct David was an adulterer, and so is she; Sanct David committed murder in slaying Uriah for his wife, and so did she; but what is this to the matter? The more wicked she be, her subjects should pray for her to bring her to the spirit of repentance .... I pray all faithful subjects to pray for their lawful magistrate, if it be the Queen. It is the Queen, as I doubt not .... No inferior subject has power to deprive or depose their lawful magistrate'.

John Row was meantime the assembly's commissioner for Galloway, but, like his predecessor, he did not come up to the assembly's exacting standards and in any case found the office a thankless one of which he sought in vain to be 'disburthened.'[48] The assembly of March 1573 repeated the inhibition against Gordon's exercise of any function in the kirk and ordained Commissioner Row to summon the bishop to appear before the next assembly to answer charges against him.[49] At the next assembly, in August, certain accusations were brought against Gordon, concerned with his support of the Marian cause and his activities as a preacher while his party held Edinburgh. The bishop made a dignified and logical reply, mainly on the legal ground that by the act of pacification he was indemnified for his offences during the civil war. 'The greatest offence,' he declared, 'that can be laid to my charge is only the preaching of the Word, which I did at command of the other authority [i.e. the Queen's party] and by election and admission of such as professed the same.' He reminded the assembly of the services rendered by many of the Marians — including Hamiltons.and Gordons — to the reformed cause in earlier years and proudly claimed that he had been 'the first that publicly preached Christ in face of the authority'. The assembly insisted on a threefold penance in sackcloth and, as the bishop had taken refuge in his diocese, ordered him to be cited at his cathedral of Whithorn. A lengthy period of bargaining ensued. The bishop did not materially recede from his position, but in March 1575 the assembly agreed to waive the sackcloth and be content with a single act of public penance at Holyrood. In the following August the assembly declared itself satisfied and exhorted the bishop to assist the commissioner of Galloway in his visitations 'for keeping good order and discipline within these bounds.[50]

Gordon did not long enjoy the reconciliation, for he died on 11 November 1575. The total value of his 'goods and gear' was under £800. He died a rather poorer man than John Knox, who had so loudly protested his preference for being a 'painful preacher of the blessed evangel' rather than a 'great bishop'. One can only comment that if Alexander Gordon's career was devoted to self-aggrandizement it had been singularly unsuccessful.

1   *Scottish Correspondence of Mary of Lorraine* (SHS) and *Papal Negotiations with Queen Mary* (SHS), both *passim*. The question of Gordon's consecration is discussed by C.G. Mortimer in 'The Scottish hierarchy in 1560', *Clergy Review*, xii, 442-50. In or about 1550 Gordon was formally described as 'marked with archiepiscopal character and consecrated' (EUL, Laing MSS III, 321, fo. 151a). Additional information is to be found in Anthony Ross, 'More about the Archbishop of Athens', *IR*, xiv, 30-37.

2   Knox, i, 129

3   *Papal Negotiations*, 28, 40, 55, 122; *ER*, xix, 451.

4   *RSS*, v, 740, 824, 1198, 1202, 2283.

5   *CSP Scot.*, i, 483

6   Books of Assumption of Thirds; *TB*, passim; *RSS*, v, 824, 1198, 1202; A and D, xli, 419, lxxvi, 202, lxxviii, 272, lxxix, 78, lxxxi, 327; Reg. Pres., i, 82.

7   Calderwood, iii, 392

8   *CSP Scot.*, i, 252, 254, 349, 372-3, 471; Knox, i, 308, 310, 335, 345, ii, 324.

9   *CSP Scot.*, i, 483.

10   *TB*, 92-3

11   Ibid., 150, 290

12   *BUK*, i, 15

13   Ibid., 28

14   Knox, ii, 72-3

15   William Scot, *Apologetical Narration* (Wodrow Soc.), 16.

16   *BUK*, i, 32, 35

17   Ibid., 38, 44, 49, 52, 65, 77

18   Ibid., 34

19   *TB*, 290

20   *RMS*, iv, 1719, 1743, 1763; *Laing Charters*, 772, 801; SRO, Morton Papers, Eccl., 23 June 1564. It seems that Tongland, rather than Whithorn, was the usual episcopal residence.

21   *BUK*, i, 31, 44.

22   *Canongate Marriage Register* (SRS), 54; HMC, *Salisbury*, xiii, 79, 81; *CSP Scot.*, ii, 258.

23   *RSS*, v, 3269, 3270.

24   *BUK*, i, 90

25   Ibid., 105; A & D, xlii, 248.

26   Keith's list of parishes (in his *Scottish Bishops*, ed. Michael Russell, 1824, pp. 311 *et seq.*) and certain maps of the diocese assign to Galloway two detached parishes — Troqueer in Kirkcudbright and Dryfesdale in Dumfriesshire. In the latter case, the parsonage was certainly appropriated to the bishopric of Glasgow, and, while this is not conclusive (for a parsonage in one diocese might be appropriated to the bishop of another), no evidence seems to justify Keith's attribution of this parish to Galloway. The parish of Troqueer was appropriated to Tongland, which in the sixteenth century was annexed to the bishopric of Galloway, but here again such evidence is not conclusive as to the diocese to which the parish belonged.

27   Alexander Vaus appears as parson of Longcastle in 1567 (*TB*, 295), but he can have been only a tacksman holding the parsonage revenues on lease from the priory of Whithorn, to which the parish was appropriated (*TDGNHAS*, 3rd ser., xxvii, 151). When Nicol Dungalson was appointed parson in 1574, the parsonage was stated to have been hitherto appropriated to Whithorn (Reg. Pres. i, 113).

28   *TDGNHAS*, 3rd ser, ix, 158 *et seq.*

29   Knox, ii, 324-5.

30   Most of the biographical information about the clergy is put together in *TDGNHAS*, xxx, 52-60; there are some additional facts in *Wigtownshire Charters* (SHS), passim.

31   *BUK*, i, 212; *APS*, iii, 72.

32 For Dundrennan we have the following names in 1559; David Johnston, Martin Foster, Nicholas Story, James Hettone (or Hutton), John Turner, Andrew Cunningham, John Wright, John Brown and Gilbert Law (Register House, Supplementary Charters); and in 1568: James Hutton, Andrew Cunningham, John Turner, Adam Cutler and David Johnston (*Protocol Book of Herbert Anderson*, ii, 64).

33 William Baillie, David Bowak, Richard Brown, Patrick Brownhill, Alexander Cairns, David Frizzell, John Galbraith, Alexander Gray, Adam Gunnoquhen, William Halkerston, Andrew Langlands, Michael Learmonth, John Sanders, William Steinsoun, John Walcar and John Wilsoun (Ailsa Charters, Box 23, Discharges and Receipts, 18 March 1558/9; Box II., Bdle. 11, 2 November, 1560).

34 *RSS*, v, 2211; *Charters of Inchaffray* (SHS), pp, xc-xcv, 160-1.

35 Eg., *RSS*, v, 1884, 2042, 2662, 2675, 3047, 3213.

36 *RPC*, i, 389; Brunton and Haig, *Senators of the College of Justice*, 129.

37 *BUK*, i, 83; Knox, ii, 188-9, 193-4; *RPC*, i, 494.

38 *BUK*, i, 31, 39-40.

39 Ibid., 52, 54.

40 Ibid., 65, 73-4.

41 Ibid., 112.

42 Register of Deeds, ix, 86.

43 In March 1568 a presentation was directed to Alexander as 'bishop and superintendent of Galloway and the chapel royal' (*RSS*, vi, 200).

44 *BUK*, i, 114.

45 Ibid., 131.

46 There are no references to Gordon as collator in the Register of Presentations, beginning in 1567; *BUK*, i, 150.

47 *TB*, 294

48 *BUK*, i, 186, 190, 200, 239, 256-7; *CSP Scot.*, iii, 609; Calderwood, iii, 91, 102-5.

49 *BUK*, i, 261, 263.

50 Ibid., 273-7, 282, 309, 319, 331, 334.

51 Edinburgh Testaments, 9 March 1575/6 and 27 April 1577.

ADAM BOTHWELL, BISHOP OF ORKNEY

The Scottish reformation came late in the day: indeed it is hard to find a country where the reformation was effected at a later date. By 1560 over forty years had passed since Luther's denunciation of Indulgences and the beginnings of the reformation in Germany, and nearly a generation had passed since Henry VIII's breach with Rome and since the establishment of a reformed church in Denmark and Norway. As ecclesiastical reform was already so widespread, it must have become apparent in Scotland that a period of decision had been reached and that affairs could not simply drift: if the existing ecclesiastical constitution was to continue, in communion with Rome, it could do so only in a more efficient form; the alternative was to repudiate Rome and accept schism, whereupon a further choice would have to be made — or perhaps dictated by circumstances — among a number of reformed models. It is an over-simplification to pose the issue as reform or no-reform; the issue was rather reform or revolution.

Because the reformation came late to Scotland, there had been ample opportunity to strengthen the traditional church structure in the hope that it would be able to withstand revolutionary assaults; the church in Scotland was exposed to no sudden and unexpected shock. Efforts at reform were indeed made, on a more serious scale than is sometimes believed. Three councils of the Scottish church, in 1549, 1552 and 1559, passed statutes designed to reform the lives of the clergy, remove abuses and provide for a certain amount of preaching; piety running along traditional lines was still active enough to produce new endowments for chaplainries and for the last of the collegiate churches, founded at Biggar in 1545; a consciousness of the necessity for an educated clergy is shown in the establishment of St. Mary's college at St. Andrews, not completed until 1552; and provision for the instruction of the people was made by the issue of Archbishop Hamilton's *Catechism*. It was, admittedly, a limited programme, and did nothing to get at one of the roots of the trouble, which was the financial starvation of the parishes and the gross over-endowment of institutions which, it was now acknowledged by all, had outlived their usefulness: but it is evidence of continuing zeal and of some awareness of the critical situation.

But there was another consequence of the lateness of the Scottish reformation: because reform had already proceeded so far in many other lands, reforming opinions had ample time to penetrate to Scotland; and it is well known how, from an act against Lutheran books in 1525 and the burning of

Patrick Hamilton for 'heresy' in 1528, there was an almost continuous chain of episodes which indicate the circulation of reforming thought in Scotland.

Both of these features, which apply to Scotland in general, apply equally to the diocese of Orkney in particular. Orkney had a share in the policy of reform from within, because in Bishop Robert Reid (1541-58), Adam Bothwell's predecessor, the diocese had as its bishop one of the outstanding churchmen of the century. Apart from his building activity, evidence of which can be seen in the Bishop's Palace, he is best known for the new constitution which he drew up for the cathedral chapter in 1544. He provided for the endowment of seven dignitaries — a provost, archdeacon, chantor, chancellor, treasurer, subdean and subchantor — seven canons, thirteen chaplains and six choristers, so that the affairs of the cathedral could be efficiently administered and its services conducted with dignity and splendour; the chancellor was to read publicly, once a week, a lecture on canon law; and the chaplain of St Peter was to be master of the grammar school.[1] This showed the bishop's interest in education, which of course was further demonstrated by the fact that on his death he left a large legacy which was intended for educational purposes and which was ultimately applied to the endowment of the university of Edinburgh.

But Bishop Reid's limitations, as well as his capacity, are plain enough. His new chapter was to be financed only by further stripping the parishes of revenues which might have been better applied to the maintenance of able parish priests to instruct the people in their faith. Public lectures by the chancellor were in themselves all very well, but a subject other than canon law might have been more beneficial to the souls of the faithful. In short, the bishop's schemes show him to have been essentially an organiser and a lawyer rather than a spiritual leader. And of course it is well known that his capacity in law led him, apparently in 1548, to the office of President of the Court of Session, and that he died in France while on a political mission in connection with the marriage of Mary, Queen of Scots, to the Dauphin of France. In short, Reid was essentially a prelate of the old regime — organiser, lawyer, politician: he was not the man to cope with imminent revolution.

But if Orkney thus had its share in the policy of what might be called conservative reform, it also had its share in the concurrent spread of reforming opinions. In 1550 a chaplain from Orkney called James Ka found it necessary to apply for a respite for his 'tenascite and pertinessite in halding of oppynionis concerning the faith contrare the tenor of actis of parliament', and he received it on condition that he 'cum within the realme of Scotland .... to remane thairin .... and use him as ane subject thairof'.[2] That curious provision does not indicate that at that time the Scottish government was not quite certain that Orkney was an integral part of the Scottish realm, for this James Ka is probably to be identified with the 'James Skea, born in Orkney', who in 1548 had been obliged to flee to England 'for fear of burning for the Word of God'.[3] At the same time, the diocese may very well have received its 'heresy' not only from the south but also from across the North Sea. Orkney's Scandinavian contacts were no longer as close as they had been, but Shetland still looked to the continent for most of its trade and there was still any number of men who were as much at home in Norway as in Shetland. Shetlanders at least, if they had any interest in all in church affairs, must have come very much under the influence of the reformation which had been an accomplished fact in Denmark and Norway since the 1530s.

The career of Bishop Bothwell, who succeeded Reid on the very eve of the Scottish crisis of 1560, can be most easily understood if an account is first given of his pedigree and family connections.[4] His father was provost of Edinburgh; his father and his uncle, Richard, were two of the original senators of the college of justice when the Court of Session was endowed in 1532; and his uncle, Richard, and his brother William held in succession the parsonage of Ashkirk in Roxburghshire, a prebend of Glasgow cathedral which was worth in 1560 the quite substantial sum of £120 annually. Equally significant were Adam Bothwell's relationships through his sisters and his mother. One sister, Margaret, married Gilbert Balfour, who became laird of Westray. Another, Janet, married Archibald Napier of Merchiston, a justice depute and the father of one of the most famous Scots of all time, John Napier of Merchiston, inventor of logarithms. Archibald Napier also had distinguished cousins. His aunt had married Sir John Melville of Raith and their family included three sons — John of Raith, Robert of Murdocairny and James of Halhill — all of whom played a conspicuous part in the political affairs of the period, and a daughter who was the mother of Sir William Kirkcaldy of Grange, one of the finest soldiers of the time. Adam Bothwell's mother, Katharine Bellenden, was sister of Thomas Bellenden of Auchnoule, justice-clerk (d. 1547) and aunt of Sir John Bellenden of Auchnoule, who succeeded his father as justice-clerk. Katharine, after the death of Adam's father, married Oliver Sinclair of Pitcairns, who figures in history as the last of James V's 'favourites'. He was a grandson of William Sinclair, earl of Orkney and Caithness and chancellor of Scotland, and a son of Sir Oliver Sinclair of Roslin; his uncle was Sir David Sinclair of Sumburgh in Shetland and he had two brothers, John and Henry, who became respectively bishops of Brechin and Ross. Oliver himself had been appointed tacksman and sheriff of Orkney by James V. He may not have been a promising step-father for a reforming bishop, as John Knox described him as 'an enemy to God'[5a], but he is the only figure in Adam Bothwell's pedigree who represents a link with the north, and one can only speculate whether connections through him had something to do with Adam's appointment to the bishopric of Orkney. Adam had his associations with this stepfather, for in 1556 he was one of the curators of Oliver's daughter.[5b] It is somewhat curious that two of Oliver's brothers became bishops and that his stepson also became a bishop, at a time when most Scottish sees were going to members of noble families; Adam Bothwell was in fact the most middle-class man on the episcopal bench.

Adam's marriage brought him into relationship with a group of individuals of higher social status. The success of protestantism in 1560 freed him from the obligation of celibacy and he married Margaret Murray, daughter of John Murray of Touchadam. John Murray's wife was Janet, a daughter of the 5th Lord Erskine and consequently a sister of the 6th Lord (who became Earl of Mar and was Regent in 1571-2), a sister of Margaret Erskine, who bore to James V the son who became Lord James Stewart, Earl of Moray, Regent in 1567-70, and a sister of Arthur Erskine, who married Magdalen Livingston, sister of Mary Livingston, one of the 'Queen's Maries'. As a nephew by marriage of the Regent Mar and a cousin by marriage of the Regent Moray he had links which may help to explain some of his activities in the late 1560s and early 1570s. The bishop's wife outlived him by fifteen years: their children were John, who succeeded his father in the abbey of Holyrood and was created Lord Holyroodhouse in 1607, five other sons and two daughters.

The future bishop was probably born in 1529. According to the epitaph on his monument in Holyrood Abbey he was in his sixty-seventh year when he died in 1593, but it seems that his parents did not marry until 1529 and that he had attained the canonical age of thirty when he was consecrated in 1559.[6] About his school and university education we have no authentic information, but of his acquisition of the degree of M.A. there can be no doubt, and there is ample evidence of the wide range of his learning, in the shape of the catalogue of the library (valued at £2000) which he possessed at his death, a list of books he presented to James VI and information about isolated volumes.[7] While the titles of the volumes which were on the bishop's bookshelves cannot give precise indications of the depth of his interest in this or that subject — any more than can be given by anyone's library — an expert examination of the books Adam possessed has demonstrated his acquaintance, to put it no higher, with Greek and Latin classics, the Greek and Latin Fathers, the works of continental reformers like Zwingli and his followers at Zurich, Calvin and Peter Martyr, Hebrew and Greek Biblical scholarship, contemporary political affairs, canon law, political thought, mathematics, medicine, botany, astronomy, rhetoric, literature in Italian, French and Spanish, and the tastes and accomplishments of gentlemen of the time.[8]

The library included also works on demonology and on sorcery, but the fact that the bishop was described as a 'sorcerer and execrable magician'[9] may reflect contemporary distrust for men skilled in, or knowledgeable about, the physical sciences and in that light may be seen as complimentary rather than derogatory. If he had indeed a reputation for dabbling in the occult it was something he shared with some distinguished contemporaries, as well as some of his kinsfolk. One of the Bellendens, it was said, 'dealt with a warlock to raise the devil' and literally died of fright when the Prince of Darkness duly appeared in his backyard in the Canongate. John Napier, the mathematician, was supposed to have a black cock as his 'familiar', and Dr Richard Napier, of an

English branch of the family, was one of the most celebrated wizards of the time.[10] Besides, John Knox (without achieving distinction as a scientist) was accused of 'necromancy'.[11]

The Bothwells seem to have had what was called a 'kindly' (that is, hereditary) interest in the parsonage of Ashkirk, but when Adam's brother William, the second Bothwell holder of it, died in 1552, he was succeeded by sir John Reid.[12] Not long seems to have elapsed, however, before the benefice was again in the possession of a Bothwell, this time Adam. In 1555 we find him linked for the first time with his future diocese, for on 21 July that year he was on the point of setting out, at the government's expense, on a journey to Orkney, in company with Mr William Mudie, who had made a trip to Orkney and Shetland earlier in the year on government business and who became chamberlain of crown property in the islands.[13]

Bishop Reid died on 14 September 1558, and on 22 March following the temporality of the see, which fell to the crown during the vacancy, was granted to Sir John Bellenden, Adam's cousin.[14] Events were clearly now moving towards Adam's promotion, and on 2 August 1559 the pope provided him to the bishopric.[15] His bulls were secured at Rome and brought home to Scotland by Gilbert Balfour, the husband of Adam's sister Margaret.[16] Bothwell was presumably consecrated bishop between the date of his provision — 2 August — and 14 October following, when he was admitted by the crown to the temporality of the see, and probably after 14 September, when he was still designated parson of Ashkirk.[17] He can barely have reached the canonical age of thirty, but he did not receive a dispensation for 'defect of age'. Although the date of the consecration cannot be precisely determined, of the fact of his consecration there can be no doubt. Consecration would normally precede admission to temporality; in his admission he is styled 'Bishop' and not 'bishop elect' as was usual before consecration; and his charters almost regularly state that they were granted in such and such a year of his consecration.[18]

Becoming a bishop in the unreformed church was an expensive business, involving heavy payments at Rome which were often met by borrowing from Italian bankers. How Bothwell met them does not appear. He cannot have been a wealthy man, though he did have private means beyond his stipend as parson of Ashkirk: he seems to have inherited from his parents rights to some property in Corstorphine, Briglands and Henderstoun, about which he was involved in litigation in 1553, 1557 and 1558,[19] and in 1560 he inherited the east toun of Dunsyre, in Lanarkshire.[20] In 1558 (that is, between 25 March 1558 and 24 March 1558/9) he borrowed 200 merks from Timothy Cagneoli, an Italian financier in the service of the Scottish crown.[21] It seems quite possible that Bellenden of Auchnoule and Gilbert Balfour, both of whom had clearly been involved in Bothwell's appointment, paid some of the costs involved and no doubt expected suitable rewards.

The diocese of which Bothwell thus became bishop was by Scottish standards neither a particularly small one nor a particularly poor one. It was divided into two archdeaconries, one for Orkney and one for Shetland — a feature shared, among Scottish dioceses, by only St. Andrews and Glasgow. In those other cases, the reason for the division was the great size of the diocese, but in Orkney the reason was presumably the fact that between the two groups of islands lay a stretch of water which neither bishop nor archdeacon would want to cross unnecessarily. It would seem that in earlier times (for which, however, our information is very scanty) the Orkney group had contained 33, or perhaps 35, parishes and Shetland 27 or perhaps 30, but by the sixteenth century a number of unions of parishes had been effected, and some of the older parishes no longer appear as independent units. The number of parishes in Orkney at the period of the reformation seems to have been not more than 24, and in Shetland the number was reduced to eleven. Even so, the diocese had more parishes than Ross, Dunblane, Caithness, Argyll, the Isles or Brechin, and was comparable, in this respect, to Dunkeld and Galloway. It is less easy to make a comparison in wealth: at the reformation, the various church revenues in Orkney, excluding those of the bishopric itself, amounted to over £1200 yearly in money, with dues in kind worth about £600 more, and in Shetland to nearly £1000, and these figures seem low until we recall that most of the other dioceses contained rich abbeys or priories which inflated their totals; the incomes of the individual livings in this diocese lay in the same range as those of other dioceses, and were, if anything, rather above than below the average.

But in Orkney, as throughout Scotland, the wealth of the church was not evenly distributed; indeed there can have been few, if any, dioceses where the diversion of parochial revenues from the parishes was carried to greater lengths than it was in Orkney. At some earlier stage, of which we have no record, the parsonages of some 23 of the original Orkney parishes had been appropriated to the bishopric. In Shetland, every parsonage was likewise annexed to the bishopric except that of Tingwall, which pertained to the archdeacon. This first stage of appropriation was less disastrous to the parishes than it might seem, because it was undoubtedly the case in Shetland, and probably so in Orkney also, that the corn teinds which formed the parsonage revenues were not wholly diverted from the parish but were divided equally between the bishop and the vicar who served in the parish. The vicarages therefore remained well endowed, and indeed, with the unions of parishes, they became, in Shetland at least, uncommonly valuable benefices. But a further, and much more serious, raid was made on the parochial revenues when Bishop Reid established his new foundation for the cathedral in 1544. It was typical of a well-meaning prelate of the unreformed church that his interest in the higher parts of the ecclesiastical structure should be carried out at the expense of the service of the parish churches. The cathedral and diocesan dignitaries were to be endowed by the appropriation to their benefices of all the parsonages in

Orkney which had hitherto remained independent, with the somewhat doubtful exception of Holy Cross, Sanday. To the dignitaries were appropriated also the majority of the vicarages. The provision which remained, after bishop and dignitaries had had their share, to furnish 'pensions' for vicars who actually served the parishes, was hopelessly inadequate. The best vicarage in Orkney — that of Sanday — was worth £30, and the others ranged down to £12; the vicarages pensionary, however, were worth only £6 or £7, with the addition of 8 bolls of victual which would be equivalent to as much again or a little more. This was at a time when a reasonable competence was somewhere in the region of £80 to £100. The position in Shetland, where there had not been a secondary stage of appropriation and the vicarages had remained independent, was incomparably better, with vicars' incomes ranging up to £120 a year. The bishopric revenues included £250 in money, with quantities of victual, marts (salted carcases of cattle), poultry, swine, butter, oil, flesh, peats, scrafish (cured saithe) and wax, valued at about £1100, giving a total income worth some £1350 in the Scots money of the time, equivalent in purchasing power to perhaps £80,000 sterling today.

The bishop, however, did not personally enjoy anything like all those revenues. The justice-clerk expected his reward for his part in arranging Adam's appointment, and the government, which had had to give its consent and formally to make the nomination at Rome, also expected its share. Thus Lord John Stewart, a half-brother of the queen, had a pension from the bishopric of £400 and the children of Sir John Bellenden ('my lord justice clerk's bairns') had another pension of the same amount — together amounting to over half the value of the bishopric; additional pensions of £200 and 160 merks were reserved to Archibald Ruthven, brother of Lord Ruthven, and Adam Murray. In all, over £1000 were going to pensioners, leaving a mere pittance for the bishop, who complained of excessive demands on him.[23]

The middle of October, when the stages in Adam's appointment to the bishopric were completed, was not the most suitable time for a journey to Orkney, and he could hardly have been blamed had he waited for the spring. It says something for him that he actually set out early in February. These were dangerous days, and tempests were not the only peril. The Scottish reformers were engaged in their struggle with the regent, Mary of Guise, and her French troops, and were enlisting the help of Elizabeth of England, who late in January 1560 sent a fleet to the Firth of Forth to prevent the arrival of French reinforcements and to cut communications between Leith, the French headquarters, and Fife, where French troops had been operating against the reformers. The new bishop, who had set out from one of the Firth of Forth ports in a small vessel, was captured on 11 February 1560 by one of the English ships near the May Island as he was doubling Fife Ness, and was taken to St Andrews, where he seems to have been detained for about six weeks.[24] On 16

March, when he was still in captivity, the lords of council, on the ground of the 'grete trublis now being in this realme and of the far distance fra thir partis to Orknay and of impediment of passing and repassing to and fra the samin', granted a commission to Bishop Adam and Alexander Dick, provost and official of Orkney, in a case between hanseatic merchants of Bergen and some Orkneymen.[25] It must have been the month of April before Bothwell reached Orkney, and there he remained for fully a year, until April 1561.[26]

Wherever Adam's sympathies may have lain — and there is no evidence whatever to indicate them — his experience off the Isle of May must have brought it home to him that the cause of France and Rome was unlikely to prevail, and it would be no surprise to him to learn, as the months of 1560 went on, of the arrival of an English army to batter at the French stronghold of Leith, the death of the Regent Mary of Guise, an arrangement for the withdrawal of both French and English troops and the meeting in August of a parliament which abolished papal authority in Scotland, forbade the celebration of the Latin mass, and adopted a reformed Confession of Faith. There is nothing to suggest that the bishop had any hesitation in committing himself to the reformed cause or that he lost much time in setting about the reform of his own diocese. He was in regular correspondence with his brother-in-law the laird of Merchiston, and communications seem to have been fairly good: the bishop wrote on 5 February 1561 acknowledging a letter of 24 December, Merchiston answered on 9 March and the bishop answered again on 25 March.[27] There are several documents demonstrating the bishop's presence in Kirkwall at various dates in June (2 and 30), September (20 and 23), October (21 and 28) and December (1 and 5) 1560 and January (19 and 28) and February (5 and 16) 1561.[28] He may have used the months of July and August for a preliminary visitation of the diocese and perhaps did more travelling later in the year, but the rest of the time he was mostly in the bishop's castle in Kirkwall ('The Yards'), attending to the finance and administration of the see.

The difficulties confronting him were enormous. There was, for one thing, his own poor health. He wrote in October 1561 that he had been 'in continual travell and labour of bodye and mynd and evill helth' ever since his arrival in Orkney, and one of his servants added that 'his lordschip was mervallis seik and beleefit nocht to haif recuverrit'.[29] There were 'cummers' or troubles — a favourite word of the bishop — stirred up by those whom he calls his 'friends', a term which he may use sarcastically or which may carry the Scottish connotation of kinsfolk. Sir John Bellenden's pension could not be paid out of the money revenues, amounting as they did to only £250, and the bishop remarked that if the price of produce continued to be as low as it had been then the payment of other pensions would not leave enough either to satisfy the justice-clerk or maintain himself. Adam warned this rapacious cousin that 'he that wald haif all, all is able to tyne'.[30] Gilbert Balfour, Adam's brother-in-law, whom the bishop had made his constable, was likewise demanding his share of the spoils, was 'continualle at debait' with Bothwell because the latter 'wald not geiff hym all that he haid' and quarrelled with his wife, the bishop's sister, on this issue.[31] Both Bellenden and Balfour, it may be recalled, had been categorised by John Knox, admittedly at an earlier stage in their careers, among 'men without God' or 'enemies to God'.[32] There was, besides, violence and disorder, brought about, so the bishop alleged, by the justice-clerk, who had instigated two Sinclair brothers, Henry and Robert, to 'loup in ane off my plaices callet Birsay, quhilk thai kepit' (that is, to seize and withhold from the bishop one of his residences); and subsequently the same 'conjuratioune', led by Henry Sinclair, beset the bishop on his way back to Kirkwall from one of his visitations: 'thair uttir purpos was to haiff alder slaine me, or taiken me.'[33] It is only right to say that there are indications of disturbances which seem to have had nothing to do directly with the bishop's 'cummers'. On 17 July 1560 George, earl of Caithness, entered into a contract with Mr Magnus Halcro of Brugh, chantor of Orkney: Magnus undertook to support the earl's interest in Orkney and take part with him should be 'invaid the cuntre of Orknay in persecutione of his auld ennymeis'; the earl on his side guaranteed protection, and if necessary a refuge in Caithness, to Magnus and thirteen named associates if they made 'persecutione or slauchter' on their enemies.[34]

Whatever personal elements may have been involved in all those 'cummers' part of the trouble undoubtedly arose from the bishop's determination to proceed with a policy of reformation. The father of those troublesome Sinclair brothers, who had been involved in a 'conjuration' against the bishop, was heard to say that 'he wald on na sort consent [that] the mess wer donne' and when the bishop took the honourable, but impolitic, course of asking for public approval of his policy, he met with a rebuff: when 'ane gret multitude of the commonis' were gathered 'at the first heid court eftyr Yeuil [Yule]', he sent a message asking 'giff thai wald be content of mutatioun of religioun and thai refusset.' Thereupon, the bishop proceeds in his account, 'I cloisset my kirk dorris and hes thoilet na mess to be said thairin sensynne; quhowbeit thai wer sua irritat thairbe, that eftyr thai haid requyret me sindrie tymes to let thaime in to that effek (i.e. to have mass) at last gaderet together in gret multitud, brocht ane preist to ane chapell hard at the scheik of the schamber quhair I wes lyand seik, and thair causset do mess, and marye certaine pairis in the auld maner. This was donne on Sonday last (2 February, 1561) quhilk I culd not stoppe without I wald haiff committit slauchter'.[35] In these incidents we have the first clear evidence that, by the beginning of 1561, the reformation was going ahead in Orkney under the bishop's direction. It was not long before news of his doings reached the south. On 5 March 1561 it was known in Edinburgh that 'the bishop of Orkney beginneth to reform his diocese, and preacheth himself'.[36]

On the 25th of that same month of March, the bishop was at Birsay and on 12 April he was once more in Kirkwall.[37] By 20 April he was on board ship in

Kirkwall roads, and by the 25th he had evidently left Orkney. He was off to France to see the queen: partly, no doubt, to lay before her in person his complaints against the justice-clerk, but partly because, like all Scots, he was intensely concerned to know what her policy would be towards the situation in Scotland and what effect her impending return would have on the country and the church. He does not seem to have reached Paris (in company with the earls of Bothwell and Eglinton and other 'noblemen and clerks') until 5 July,[39] and cannot have spent long there; apparently he returned to Scotland when Mary herself returned on 19 August, for news of her arrival and his had reached Kirkwall by 28 August.

In spite of the machinations of the justice-clerk and others, the opposition to the reformation, and his serious illness, the bishop had succeeded, during his residence in his diocese in 1560-61, in laying the foundations of the organisation of a reformed church. The purely technical difficulties had been considerable, for if he had had to rely on the existing parish benefices, the vicarages and vicarages pensionary, it would have been quite beyond his power to provide emoluments for an adequate reformed ministry. The way was open, however, for a minor revolution in the ecclesiastical structure. The utility of cathedral dignitaries was now open to question, while the emphasis of the reformation was on the parish ministry, and the bishop therefore hit on the plan of making the dignitaries serve as ministers in the parishes from which their revenues derived. In adopting this policy, Bothwell was as typical of the reformed church as Reid had been of the unreformed, and in a sense he reversed Reid's work of diverting revenues from parochial purposes.

Of the clergy whom Bothwell found in office, quite the most reliable at this stage seems to have been James Annand, who had been prebendary of St John since, at latest, 1558, and who, if not already chancellor of the diocese, was at once appointed to that dignity by the new bishop. The chancellory was endowed with the parsonage and vicarage of our Lady in Sanday, the vicarage of Holy Cross and St Colm in Sanday and the vicarage of North Ronaldsay; and Annand also acquired the parsonage of Holy Cross in Westray. In the islands of Sanday, North Ronaldsay and Westray, therefore, Annand in 1561 commenced a ministry which lasted until about 1584.[41] Magnus Halcro, who, as chantor (an office which he had held since 1555) was parson and vicar of Orphir, vicar of Stennes and vicar of Firth, certainly accepted the reformation, for he presently made his appearance as a bridegroom. The facts that the parishes of Orphir, Stennes and Firth, almost alone among the parishes of Orkney, have no name of a reformed clergyman attached to them until 1567, and that in 1561 Halcro did not pay his third of Stennes, suggest that he may have been intended to serve, and perhaps did serve for a time, in those parishes, but he does not seem to have been promising material for a shepherd of souls, partly because of his involvement in local feuds (which had led to his league with the earl of Caithness in 1560, mentioned above) and partly because he was ultimately excommunicated for adultery.[42] It seems possible that Peter Houston, who had been subdean and parson of Hoy since 1544, acted as minister in Hoy for a few years until his death in 1566. Magnus Strang, the subchantor, may have been similarly responsible for the parishes of Sandwick and Stromness, but he died in 1562. Alexander Dick, provost of Orkney since 1554, drew his revenues from the parsonage and vicarage of Our Lady in South Ronaldsay, the vicarage of St Peter there and the vicarage of Burray. He is not recorded as minister in those islands until 1574, and it may be that he was a late and reluctant convert to protestantism. [43a]

Among the parish clergy, too, there seem to have been those who at once threw in their lot with the reformed cause and started to act as readers in 1561. Stronsay and Eday enjoyed the ministrations of James Maxwell, who had for twenty years or more been vicar of Stronsay, prebendary of St Katharine and chaplain of Holy Cross and who was to give another thirty years or so of service in the reformed church. There is good reason to believe that Gavin Watt, vicar pensioner of Deerness, David Anderson, vicar pensioner of Evie, John Duncanson, vicar pensioner of Sandwick and Stromness, Laurence Young, vicar of Rousay, John Malison, vicar pensioner of Walls, William Brown, vicar of Shapinsay, also began to serve as readers in 1561.

In Shetland, the bishop was fortunate in having from the outset a firm supporter, Jerome Cheyne, in the key position of archdeacon. A brother of Thomas Cheyne, of Esslemont, in Aberdeenshire, he had first appeared in history in 1546, when 'Jerome Cheyne, clerk' and James, his brother, were accused in the burgh court of Aberdeen of assaulting two other men. Jerome was a notary, and by 1547 had become parson of Torry in Fife, a living which he held until 1569. He was presented to the archdeaconry of Shetland in 1554 and was apparently a valued servant of Bishop Reid, whom he accompanied on his fatal mission to France. [43b] Whether Bishop Bothwell visited Shetland on his first stay in his diocese must remain uncertain, but he did at this time take the first step towards reforming the church in Shetland by appointing Archdeacon Cheyne to serve as 'minister in these parts'. Two Shetland parish priests — Magnus Murray, vicar of Walls, and James Fallowsdale, vicar of Yell — enjoyed similar recognition, as readers, in 1562, but it is not known whether they had acted in 1561. Fallowsdale had held his vicarage since 1542, and Murray was probably in possession of his Shetland vicarage (as well as the vicarage of St Ola in Orkney) when Bishop Bothwell succeeded to the see. In no other case does it appear likely that the existing holder of a Shetland benefice conformed and continued to serve his cure in the reformed church. In Unst and Sandsting the holder clearly did not serve; in most of the other parishes a vacancy seems to have given Bishop Bothwell the opportunity to make a new appointment in 1561 or 1562.[44]

To supplement the existing staff of the diocese, and to fill benefices as they fell vacant, Bishop Bothwell had brought in his train men who were in full

sympathy with his policy and who shared with the survivors of the older regime
the task of carrying through the reformation in the north. The outstanding
name among them is that of Gilbert Foulsie, a priest from Aberdeenshire who
had evidently formerly been a monk; he came north as secretary to the bishop
and was appointed to the prebend of St John (resigned by James Annand) on 28
January 1560/1. Not much later, and probably during the bishop's first visit,
Foulsie was promoted to the archdeaconry of Orkney. He thus became the
bishop's lieutenant for Orkney, but he also acted as minister of Birsay and
Harray, the parishes from which the archdeacon's revenues came.[45] Also in the
bishop's train came his kinsman — a nephew, though his precise place in the
family tree is not determined — Francis Bothwell, an ex-friar. He cannot have
been Francis, son of William Bothwell, burgess of Edinburgh who was
prebendary of St Laurence in 1567, but presumably the Francis who had
matriculated at St Andrews in 1537 and must have been little older than the
bishop. He now became prebendary of St Augustine by 21 October 1560 and
treasurer of the cathedral not long after. The treasureship was founded on
benefices in Stronsay, Eday and Fara, and it seems likely that Francis
commenced his spiritual oversight of those islands in 1561.[46a] William Lauder,
a notary who acted in Glasgow in 1558 and a Master of Arts,[46b] another early
associate of Bishop Bothwell, appears to have succeeded Gilbert Foulsie as the
bishop's secretary but did not immediately receive preferment or undertake
ministerial duties, though in due course he became vicar and minister of Yell
and Fetlar.[46c]

James Alexander, another clerk on the bishop's staff, never became a
minister, but appears later as commissary of Orkney. Possibly a bishop who was
himself something of a lawyer had a peculiar regard for men with legal
qualifications or interests. We certainly find him showing favour to another
notary, this time one who was not a newcomer to the diocese — John Gifford,
who had been in Kirkwall since 1553 and a vicar choral of the cathedral since
1554. As a notary, he witnessed one of Bothwell's charters in 1560; very soon
afterwards he was vicar of Northmavine, in Shetland, to which he had
evidently been appointed by the bishop and which he long served, first as a
reader and later as a minister.[47a]

Adam Bothwell's proceedings in his diocese were approved — and suitably
recompensed — by central authority. It seems that it was not until December
1562 that a committee of the privy council, on recommendations submitted by
the superintendents and their courts, allocated stipends and other payments
from the thirds which were being collected.[47b] This meant that remuneration
was given retrospectively for the accounting year 1561 (i.e. 25 March 1561 - 24
March 1561/2), and that is why, as already mentioned, it is sometimes difficult
to be confident about what had been happening in 1560 and 1561. However,
the general practice was agreed, by a commonsense arrangement to avoid
taking money away as third and returning it as stipend, to allow holders of

benefices who served in the reformed church simply to retain their thirds instead of having them uplifted by the collectors. Now, in 1561 Adam Bothwell had not paid his third because he evidently thought that he was entitled to retain it, although no formal permission had been given him to do so. But in the Account for 1562, we find that he received official recognition both for that year and also, retrospectively, for 1561:- 'the soume of £300 allowed to Adam, Bishop of Orknay, for his visitatioun, ovirsycht and lawbouris tane upoun the kirkis of Orknay and Zetland in place of a superintendent; and uther £300 allowed to the same bischop for the 1xi (1561) yeir for the caus forsaid, quhilk wes not allowed to the comptare in his comptis the said yeir bot rested on the said bischop'.[48] That is the evidence that Bothwell's work was effectively acceptable to what may be called the central authority, but as the early records of the general assembly are extremely defective it is impossible to say at what point the assembly first defined its attitude to the bishop. The first *recorded* relevant act does not come until June 1563, when Bothwell, with the bishops of Galloway and Caithness, was commissioned to act as superintendent in his diocese,[49] and the same arrangement evidently continued for some years. The bishop attended most of the meetings of the assembly from June 1563 to December 1566 and must have been thought a valuable member, for he was appointed to sit on a commission for revising the Book of Discipline in December 1563 and on committees in 1565 and 1566.[50] We find the assembly acting in 1563 as a court of appeal from a sentence in a case of divorce heard by the bishop, with the 'eldaris and deacons of Orknay', on 8 August 1562.[51]

In the years after his initial visit to Orkney in 1560-1 the bishop was in his diocese much more often than has usually been believed. Charters issued by him make it probable that he was in Orkney in June 1562, July 1563, October 1564 and August 1566.[52] Possibly those charters are not in themselves conclusive evidence of the bishop's presence in the north on the dates on which they purport to have been granted, but an examination of Bothwell's itinerary makes it seem likely that he visited his diocese in the summer or autumn nearly every year, and confirms the charter evidence. It is to be noted, too, that Bothwell was subsequently criticised for visiting his kirks as a commissioner of the assembly (that is, after 1563) only from Lammas to Hallowmass[54] (that is, from August to October), and that statement agrees with the dates when he appears to have been in Kirkwall in 1564 and 1566. The bishop claimed later that as a commissioner he had visited all the kirks in his diocese twice, to the hazard of his life in dangerous storms on the seas,[55] and from this it has been carelessly inferred that he visited his diocese only twice; but that does not necessarily follow, for it is unlikely that he would attempt to visit every kirk each time he was in Orkney, and in any event he had made at least one visitation (in 1560-61) before he had been commissioned by the Assembly.

From 1564 the bishop's interests were to some extent diverted from ecclesiastical affairs, and his diocese saw less of him. He was admitted an extraordinary lord of session on 14 January 1563/4 and an ordinary lord on 13 November 1565. 'Some of the brethren' in the general assembly thought it improper that he should combine this judicial office with his office in the church,[56] but the assembly did not pounce on him with a condemnation. Adam's regular presence in court can be traced from January 1563/4 until July, after which he was absent until November — one reason for believing that he paid a visit to Orkney in that period. From November 1564 until the summer of 1567 he seems never to have been long absent from court during term-time. Even as an absentee from the diocese, however, he could still do good work for the reformed church by appointing ministers to benefices,[57] and the witness lists of his charters show that the Orcadian clergy not infrequently visited him in Edinburgh and no doubt discussed policy with him.

The bishop's visit to Orkney in the summer 1562 had possibly marked a second stage in the organisation of the reformed church in the diocese and had resulted in the provision of a more adequate staff for the parishes than had been possible in 1561. The principal newcomer in Orkney was Jerome Tulloch, subchantor in succession to Magnus Strang, who was still in office early in 1562 and presumably died in the same year. The subchantory was endowed from the parsonages of Stromness and St Colm in Sanday, and, as Sanday was in the care of James Annand, Tulloch was assigned to the charge of Sandwick and Stromness, where he ministered from 1562 onwards. Thomas Beinstoun, vicar of Rousay and minister there, may also have been a new recruit. The other ministers now in office were Foulsie who had charge possibly of Kirkwall, certainly of Birsay and Harray; Francis Bothwell in Stronsay, Eday and Fara; James Annand in Westray, Sanday and North Ronaldsay; possibly Dick in South Ronaldsay and Burray; and perhaps Thomas Stevenson (who superseded the scandalous Magnus Halcro) in Orphir, Stennes and Firth (although he does not appear in record until 1567). In addition, there were eight readers or exhorters, some of whom, as we saw, probably acted in 1561:- Nicol Cragy (Holm), Thomas Rattray (Burray and South Ronaldsay), Gavin Watt (St Andrews and Deerness), John Duncanson (Stromness and Sandwick), David Anderson (Evie), John Malison (Walls), Laurence Young (Rousay) and William Brown (Westray and Sanday). Very nearly all, if not quite all, the parishes were now enjoying the ministrations of a reformed clergyman of one rank or another. In Shetland 1562 saw less change, unless Magnus Murray and James Fallowsdale were accessions to the ranks of the reformed clergy at this point rather than in 1561.

The years 1563-6 saw some changes in the personnel of the reformed clergy in Orkney, but few additions to their number. Thomas Taylor, another reader, relieved William Brown of the charge of Sanday (with which he served also North Ronaldsay); Duncan Ramsay became reader at South Ronaldsay and Burray, leaving Thomas Rattray free to devote himself to Shapinsay; and John Sadler became reader at Kirkwall.

The year 1567 is one for which we have singularly full information, and it shows the position achieved when Bishop Bothwell's work was in its final stages. There were now seven, or perhaps nine, ministers in Orkney:- Archdeacon Foulsie (Kirkwall); Donald Walker (Birsay and Harray); Donald Bruce (Deerness); Thomas Stevenson (Orphir, Stennes and Firth, perhaps with oversight of Evie and Rendall); Jerome Tulloch (Sandwick and Stromness); Thomas Beinstoun (Rousay); presumably Francis Bothwell (Stronsay); James Annand (Westray, Sanday and North Ronaldsay); and possibly Alexander Dick (South Ronaldsay and Burray). The only parishes which do not seem to have been supervised by a minister were Hoy and Walls. There were also thirteen readers: John Sadler (Kirkwall); Robert Stewart (Birsay and Harray); Gavin Watt (Deerness); Nicol Craigie (Holm); Archibald Reid (probably Evie and Rendall); Laurence Young (Rousay); Thomas Fleming (Hoy); John Malison (Walls); James Maxwell (Stronsay); William Brown (Westray); Thomas Taylor (Sanday and North Ronaldsay); Thomas Rattray (Shapinsay); and Edward Inkster (South Ronaldsay and Burray). In Shetland by this time there were two ministers — Jerome Cheyne and William Lauder; and nine readers (William Taylor, James Fallowsdale, Matthew Litstar, John Gifford, George Duff, John MacQuhaill, William Watson, William Philp, and John Crab). The total for the diocese was over 30, giving an officiant of some kind in almost every parish.

The law and practice of the church being what they were, all those ministers and readers must have been examined and admitted by the bishop or by someone whom he deputed to act for him (very likely Foulsie in Orkney and Cheyne in Shetland),[58] for in that period no one except the bishop had authority to admit ministers and readers. That the achievement was creditable would undoubtedly emerge if a comparison were made with other parts of Scotland, for it may be questioned if any other area was much better staffed. It may well add to Bothwell's credit that the position achieved by 1567 was essentially unchanged in 1574 and 1576. The numbers of clergy — seven ministers and fourteen readers in Orkney in 1574 and 1576 — showed no increase. Not only so, but the men in office were still in the main men whom the bishop had appointed. In short, although the bishop was criticised, his withdrawal from the administration of the diocese led to no spectacular improvement.

Taking it that Bishop Bothwell's reorganisation of his diocese was completed by 1567, this is the point at which to assess the character of the reformation in that northern area, a reformation carried through by a bishop who had been appointed before 1560, with the assistance very largely of clergy likewise already in office. All the indications are that the reformation was moderate in character and avoided needless dislocation. Continuity in personnel is most impressive, for it may be questioned whether there was any other diocese in Scotland where so few clergy did not accept the reformation. Out of 34 Orkney clergy who are certainly known, or who may be strongly presumed, to have been in office in 1560, 14 continued to serve in the parishes attached to their benefices, and four or five others may have done so; four more served in the reformed church in other spheres of duty; only seven appear not to have served; and there are four about whom no evidence has come to light. The only clerics who are known to have been alive in1560 and who did not serve seem to have been John Anderson, vicar of Evie; James Laing, vicar pensioner of Stennes; John Maxwell, parson of Lady parish, Sanday (who was dead by 1565); Alexander Scott, parson of Westray (dead by 1566); Magnus Strang, the subchantor (died 1562); Nicol Tulloch, vicar of Westray; John Reid, vicar of Fetlar; and Andrew Hill, vicar of Unst. Thomas Richardson, prebendary of St Katharine, certainly conformed, although he did not serve; George Gifford, one of the vicars choral, acted likewise,[59] and the same may be true of some others. Some may have been aged and infirm, some of them pluralists whose main interest did not lie in Orkney, e.g. Nicol Tulloch.[60] Some took time to make up their minds: Dick, the provost, and William Peirson, parson of Holy Cross, Sanday, are not recorded as ministers until 1574, by which date they were in danger of deprivation if they did not accept the reformed confession of faith (though there was still no penalty for failure to serve).

The mild nature of the Orcadian reformation can be illustrated also by the absence of material destruction. The deliberate damage done to church buildings throughout Scotland generally has indeed often been grossly exaggerated, but in Orkney there is no evidence of any damage at all, and the cathedral of St Magnus is conspicuous proof not only that there was no deliberate destruction but that there was not even the grave neglect which led to the decay of cathedrals elsewhere. It may be, further, that the changes in public worship were less radical in Orkney than elsewhere. Of the bishop's own views on this subject we have only one scrap of evidence — the fact that he disagreed with those who opposed the anointing of King James at his coronation in 1567. There are, however, other indications that some conservatism may have tempered the changes made in church services. When, in 1567, Bishop Bothwell fell out of favour with the general assembly and a kind of indictment listed all the accusations which could be unearthed to his discredit, one of the counts was that his nephew Francis, the ex-friar, was 'a papist'.[61] This cannot have been literally true of a man whose third had been officially allowed to him for his service in the reformed church, but it could mean only that Francis had been less austere than most Scottish reformers in rejecting old observances and ritual. There is also the case of Alexander Dick the provost. He was accused in November 1567 — a month before the indictment of the bishop — of saying mass in contravention of the proclamation which had been issued by Queen Mary on her return to Scotland in August 1561, and also of 'adulteration of religion'.[62] Now, there was nothing ambiguous about saying mass, though the accusation might have been dredged up from an offence some years old, but that phrase 'adulteration of religion' was used many years later of Archbishop Patrick Adamson — 'filthily adulterating the state of public prayer'[63] — when he had been guilty of nothing worse than using the English Prayer Book. It may very well be that in Bishop Bothwell's diocese the Prayer Book remained in use after it had been displaced generally by the Book of Common Order and that the Christian Year continued to be more regularly observed than it was in other parts of Scotland.

Reviewing the whole situation, we have in Orkney a reformation carried through by a bishop who had been appointed before the reformation, with the assistance very largely of clergy already in office: carried through, too, without violence and apparently by men of moderate views. The proceeding was not in conformity with the Scottish reformation as it is usually understood, and in some ways more resembles the English reformation; but the parallel of the Lutheran reformation in Denmark and Norway may suggest that the racial characteristics of the people of Orkney and Shetland made that type of reformation peculiarly acceptable to them. Orkney shared with other northern lands the further feature that the reformation there was complete, and that no indigenous Roman Catholicism survived in the islands.

But if the advance of the reformation in Orkney seems thus to have encountered no grave obstacles after its initial stages, there were plenty of 'cummers', as the bishop called them, arising from other causes. There was an unseemly incident in Kirkwall in September 1561. Alexander Dick, the provost of the cathedral, along with Edward Sinclair, brother of Sinclair of Roslin, Francis Bothwell the ex-friar, sir Duncan Ramsay, sir Magnus Strang and a number of others were accused of 'convocation and gathering of our sovereign lady's lieges to the number of 80 persons' and issuing out of the cathedral to seek Henry Sinclair of Strome and Mr William Mudy 'for their slaughter'. Whatever lay behind this, and how far it was related to some of the disturbances of the previous year, is not clear; and as the clergy named as taking part do not look like a homogeneous group of partisans on one side or the other it is unlikely that ecclesiastical issues were involved; but it is clear that a lot of bad blood persisted.[64] 'Cummers' which directly affected the bishop issued rather in the less spectacular field of litigation, which seems to have been almost incessant. He had suits, usually with merchants in Kirkcaldy, Leith or Edinburgh, about the disposal of the butter, oil and bere which came in among his revenues, and about the ships in which they were carried south; with his brother-in-law Gilbert Balfour about the lands of Birsay and other matters; and with William Sinclair of Dunbeath about the duties of some of the bishopric lands in Caithness.[65]

Responsibility for the management of the revenues should have fallen largely on the bishop's chamberlain, but Bothwell seems to have been unfortunate with his chamberlains, who gave him as much trouble as they might have been expected to save him. Gilbert Balfour, of whom no more need be said here, held the office of chamberlain in 1561, no doubt as part of a bargain connected with the bishop's appointment. Thomas Tulloch of Fluris succeeded. In March 1561, before he became chamberlain, Tulloch had a suit with the bishop, Gilbert Balfour and Patrick Cullane about property in Noltland, and in June following he was involved with the bishop, Balfour, William Lauder and others in a dispute over the bishopric fruits and some moveable goods.[70] Then on 29 July Tulloch sued the bishop, Balfour (still at that time chamberlain), Magnus Strang, the subchantor, John Brown, burgess of Kirkwall, John Balfour, Gilbert's brother, sir John Gifford, Patrick and John Culane, for the spoliation of divers goods from his property in Kirkwall on 18-24 May 1560, and a similar suit on the same date reverted to the dispute over Noltland.[71] Tulloch seems to have proved a very unsatisfactory chamberlain, for the bishop had a long litigation in 1564 to try to make him account for the two years during which he had held the office, and in 1565 Tulloch, after being in dispute with Patrick Bellenden about the bishopric account books, bonds and discharges for 1562 and 1563, was ordered by the Court of Session to produce his books before James Alexander, commissary of Orkney, and Alexander Dick, provost of the cathedral. The Bishop's troubles with his next chamberlain, William Lauder, which did not reach crisis until 1569, will be explained later.[72]

It looked in 1564 as if the bishop's financial 'cummers' were over, for there was a phase of settlement of differences. On 10 March a decreet arbitral was drawn up between the bishop and Gilbert Balfour of Westray: Gilbert was to enjoy his lands of Westray, but to pay his dues for them, according to his charter of 30 June 1560, but he was to give up the lands of Birsay and Marwick, which the bishop had redeemed, in return for 1000 merks; he was also to surrender the discharges for Lord John Stewart's pension for terms preceding September 1561, which Gilbert had paid to Lord John.[75] On 21 June an interesting case came before the Court of Session: James Tullo in Schapinschaw, Robert Blak in Laverik, John Smith in Birsay, Magnus Robesoun in Schapay and the remanent indwellers in the bishopric of Orkney had raised an action against Bishop Bothwell and Patrick Bellenden, the sheriff, alleging that both claimed jurisdiction over them; judgement was given for the bishop.[76] On 1 July a decreet arbitral was recorded whereby William Maitland, apparent of Lethington, as arbiter, gave his decision on the disputes between the bishop and the justice-clerk. It had been agreed by a contract dated at Edinburgh on 4 June 1562 that Bothwell, who was bound to pay Bellenden £400 yearly, would, as long as the bishopric was burdened with a pension of £400 to Lord John Stewart and one of £200 to Archibald Ruthven, pay 20 lasts of victual called 'cost', 12 barrels of flesh and 6 barrels of butter; now, Lord John being dead, the bishop was to pay £200 to Bellenden in addition to the said victual, and for the sum he was to assign certain duties. Bellenden, on his side, was to make no other claims, but the bishop was to set the lands of Birsay and others to him in feu.[77] Another decreet arbitral by Maitland, made on 30 June 1564 and registered on

7 July, was between the bishop and Patrick Bellenden of Stennes, Sir John's brother and sheriff of Orkney. All manner of injuries, quarrels and offences were to be forgiven and they were to live in perfect love and Christian charity. The bishop was to set in feu to Patrick the lands of Stennes, viz. Lurmisden, Culstaine and Housbister, the 'hill' of Anehallow in the parish of Rousay and the lands of Evie; and to give a tack for 19 years of the teind sheaves of the queen's lands in Evie (pertaining to Our Lady Stouk); Patrick was to restore to Gilbert Foulsie the fruits of his benefice which he had intromitted with in times past.[77] At the end of that same month of July a minor suit came before the Court of Session, by Sir John Bellenden of Auchnoule against Bishop Bothwell, Gilbert Balfour, fiar of Westray, and Margaret Bothwell, his spouse: Sir John was infeft in feu, by resignation of the said Gilbert and Margaret in the bishop's hands, in 'Birsay abon the hyll, Birsay besowth, Birsay benorth', with the mill, Skaldenfra, Hundland, Solsister and Marvik, on the conditions to which Gilbert was astricted, as recorded in the 'Register of Orknay'. Bellenden desired an extract from that register, but Gilbert Foulsie, its keeper, had refused to give him one until action was brought against him. The extract had now been produced, and the lords ordered it to be transumed.[79]

However, all the financial complications, troublesome though they must have been to the bishop, were succeeded before long by a new and graver series of 'cummers' arising from his officiating at the marriage of Queen Mary to James Hepburn, earl of Bothwell, on 15 May 1567. For this action the bishop has been much blamed, both at the time and since, but it seems that there is something to be said for him. What was the situation? Ever since Mary's return from France in 1561 the situation had been unstable and the reformed church in an insecure position; in 1565 and 1566 the indications were that things were going to be still worse, for the queen's policy seemed to be heading towards a papalist reaction and the reformed church was receiving very unfavourable treatment, financially and otherwise. Towards the end of 1566 there came a sudden change in the royal policy, the likely motives for which have been discussed elsewhere.[79] Generous financial provision was now made for the ministers. On top of this came the murder of Darnley and Mary's marriage to Bothwell. Of course it was a scandalous marriage, to the man universally believed to be the murderer of the queen's late husband. But there were other considerations: the earl of Bothwell, with all his faults, was an unwavering protestant; the queen followed up her financial generosity to the ministers by an act rescinding laws against the reformed church and indeed taking that church under her protection, and she consented to be married according to the reformed rite — 'at a preaching, be Adam Bodowell, Bischop of Orkeney, ... according to the ordour of the reformed religion, and not in the chapell at the mess, as was the king's (Darnley's) marriage'.[80] It should be said that by this time Bishop Bothwell seems to have been closely associated with the royal court and even the royal household, for in the previous autumn, when Darnley had paid a brief visit to Holyrood and had not slept with his wife, he had spent the night in a bed belonging to the bishop of Orkney.[81] But it is not unrealistic to speculate that with what seemed to be an alliance between the queen and the kirk, there appeared a distinct prospect of new and better times for the reformed cause, and Adam Bothwell may well have conceived it to be his duty, and even a privilege, to be one of the instruments in helping to bring about such a happy conclusion. Unlike those who have condemned him, he did not know what the sequel was to be — how within a matter of weeks Mary would be deposed in favour of her infant son and the earl of Bothwell would be a fugitive from the wrath of the confederate lords.

This revolution did, however, open up prospects at least as pleasing to one of the bishop's principles as any developments which might have ensued from the Bothwell marriage, and it is not surprising that the celebrant of that marriage presently took part in the coronation of the bride's supplanter and joined in the pursuit of the bridegroom. His actions are perfectly explicable on the simple assumption that he was all along seeking the good of the reformed church in which he had been active since 1560.

The bishop was appointed one of the persons who, on 29 July 1567, received Mary's demission of the crown.[82] On the same day the new king's coronation took place at Stirling. Along with the superintendents of Angus and Lothian, Bishop Bothwell crowned the king; the bishop anointed him on his head, shoulder-blades and hands, 'saying certain prayers before in the English tongue', and at the end of the service gave the blessing. The sermon was preached by John Knox.[83]

The earl of Bothwell, meanwhile, had made for Orkney, of which the queen had made him duke. Gilbert Balfour refused to allow him to establish himself at either Kirkwall or Noltland, and he moved on to Shetland. In August, only a matter of days after the new king's coronation, an expedition left Dundee in pursuit of the fugitive. It was commanded by Kirkcaldy of Grange, and he took with him his cousin the bishop, who had the advantage of knowing the islands (though, it was to turn out, he did not know the waters surrounding them well enough), he could use his authority to obtain local assistance for the pursuing force, he was a Lord of Session with a knowledge of law which might prove useful. This adventure led to the most picturesque incident in Adam Bothwell's career. The pursuers came on the earl of Bothwell's ships in Bressay Sound, in Shetland; the earl himself was ashore, but his ships fled northwards. Kirkcaldy almost overtook them outside the north mouth of the sound, but Bothwell's pilot steered close to a hidden rock and Kirkcaldy's ship, pressing on in the chase, ran aground. The incident was related in a vivid manner by Mark Napier in his *Memoirs of Merchiston*, and his account deserves to be reprinted as an example of Victorian historiography at its most spirited.

'It was not long before two vessels were descried cruising off the east coast of Shetland, where currents, tides and whirlpools threatened destruction to the most skilful navigator. These vessels were the Duke of Orkney's [Bothwell's], on the look out, and manned by desperate seamen. Grange, who commanded the swiftest of the government ships, shot ahead, and approached Bressay Sound, through which the pirates steered. Onward pressed their pursuers, and every nerve was strained on board the *Unicorn,* Grange's ship, to gain their object. The manoeuvre of the fugitives would have done credit to the more practised days of the Red Rover. So close was the chase, that, when the pirate escaped by the north passage of the sound, Grange came in by the south, and continued the chase northward. But the fugitives were familiar with those narrow and dangerous seas. They knew how lightly their own vessels could dash through the boiling eddy that betrayed a sunken rock, and discerned at a glance what would be the fate of their bulky pursuers if they dared to follow in their desperate track. They steered accordingly upon breakers; and though the keel grazed the rocks, their vessel glided through the cresting foam, and shot into a safer sea. Grange ordered every sail to be set to impel the *Unicorn* in the very same path. In vain his more experienced mariners remonstrated. The warlike baron, as if leading a charge of horse in the plains of Flanders, rushed on the breakers, and instantly his gallant ship was a wreck — there being just time to hoist out a boat and save the ship's company and soldiers. As it was, one warrior heavily armed still clung to the wreck, and, the boat being already on its way deeply laden, it seemed impossible to save this being from destruction. His cries reached them, but were disregarded; another instant of delay and he had perished, when, collecting all his energies, he sprung with a desperate effort into the midst of the crowded boat, causing it to reel with his additional weight, encumbered as he was with a corslet of proof; which, says Godscroft, who records the incident, was thought a strange leap, especially not to have overturned the boat. Who would have surmised that this athletic man-at-arms, the last to quit the wreck, was a bishop! — the bishop who had so lately joined the hand of him he pursued, with that of Queen Mary! — the very bishop who a month before had poured the holy oil on the infant head of James VI and stood proxy for the extorted abdication of that monarch's mother. It was Adam Bothwell, Bishop of Orkney. The rock from which he leapt can be seen at low water, and is called the Unicorn to this day.'

The Unicorn Rock is indeed marked on the chart, which states that it 'dries', but I have not met anyone who has seen it even with the lowest tide, though of course the sea can be seen breaking over it. Anyone who wants to escape the fate of Kirkcaldy's *Unicorn* should note that the rock's position can be fixed by taking bearings of Score Head over Green Holm and the Ward of Clett (in Whalsay) over the Mull of Eswick. The pursuit of Bothwell, fruitless though it was, had to be paid for. The fitting out of the ships cost the lords £600 and a further £1228 was disbursed by the Collector of Thirds, who also paid £93 for provisions bought while the ships' companies were ashore in Shetland. Andrew Lamb, the well-known Leith merchant, provided powder, bullets and other articles, for which the Regent Moray promised him £2500, but 1000 merks of that sum were still owing to him in 1579, when he presented a petition to the Auditor of the Thirds asking for an assignation of quantities of meal and wheat from the abbey of Arbroath, and this was granted.[84]

Adam Bothwell had given proof of his readiness to risk even his life in the cause of King James and the reformed church, but it is clear that a serious breach had opened between him and the general assembly. The reason is by no means apparent. It is true that the standard of efficiency which the reformed church demanded of its administrators was a high one — so high, indeed, that few attained it, and almost every superintendent and bishop was under censure at one time or another. But it was a time when the king's party was singularly unsure of itself and when many of its supporters were not to be relied on, so the root cause of the bishop's troubles may have been nothing more than a general atmosphere of suspicion; equally, there may have been personal or family feuds at work which are concealed from us, and we may especially suspect the influence of Lord Robert Stewart, Commendator of Holyrood and feuar of Orkney, who wanted, by fair means or foul, to oust the bishop from Orkney and establish complete control there. At any rate, Adam Bothwell had not attended the meetings of the general assembly in June and July 1567, and when it met again in December of that year a series of accusations against him was produced: his visitation had not been sufficiently conscientious; his interests were diverted by his place as a judge in the Court of Session; he had in his company Francis Bothwell, 'a papist'; and he had solemnised the marriage of the queen to the earl of Bothwell, contrary to an act against marrying a divorced adulterer. The bishop was deprived 'from all function in the ministry'. Yet on every charge except the last, where the assembly was no doubt technically in the right, the bishop had a good defence; his health, he said, made it impossible to 'remain in Orkney all the year, by reason of the evil air and the weakness of his body'; he denied that Francis Bothwell was a papist; and he reminded the assembly that it had approved of his acceptance of office as a lord of session.[85] When the assembly met again, in July 1568, the bishop was restored to his functions, on condition that he made a public profession of his fault in celebrating the queen's marriage[86] — a condition which may suggest that his defence was considered satisfactory on the other charges.

The bishop next demonstrated his zeal for the cause of King James by taking part in the negotiations which, the king's party hoped, would lead to a condemnation of Queen Mary and the recognition by Elizabeth of King James. He was a member of a commission which included the Earl of Moray (now regent), the Earl of Morton, the Commendator of Dunfermline (Robert Pitcairn) and Lord Lindsay and which was accompanied by professional assessors among whom were George Buchanan and William Maitland of Lethington. The party left Edinburgh at the end of September 1568, arrived in York on 3 October, moved on to London before mid-November and were authorised to return to Scotland on 12 January 1568/9 — a fairly prolonged absence for Bothwell from his usual 'cummers'. The bishop figured in a spirited incident at Westminster. Moray had an 'eik' or additional accusation of Mary which he was reluctant to produce until he received certain formal guarantees from Elizabeth, but he was frustrated by the agility of Bishop Bothwell, whose spectacular 'loup' out of the *Unicorn* had not been forgotten. Sir James Melville relates in his memoirs that when the Duke of Norfolk asked Moray for the 'eik', the Regent 'desired again the assurance of the conviction [of Mary] by writing and seal, as is said. It was answered again that the Queen's Majesty's word, being a true princess, was sufficient. Then all the council cried out, "Would he mistrust the Queen, who had given such proof of her friendship to Scotland?" The Regent's council cried out also in that same manner. Then Secretary Cecil asked if they had the accusation there. "Yes", says Mr John Wood; and with that he plucks it out of his bosom, "But I will not deliver it till Her Majesty's hand-writ and seal be delivered to my Lord Regent for what he demands." Then the Bishop of Orkney snatcheth the writ out of Mr John Wood's hand. "Let me have it," says he, "I shall present it." Mr John ran after him, as if he would have it again or torn his clothes. Forward goes the bishop to the council table, and gives in the accusation. Then said to him my Lord William Howard, chamberlain of England, "Well done, Bishop Turpy; thou art the smartest fellow among them all; none of them will make thy leap good;" scorning him for his leaping out of the laird of Grange's ship ... The Regent ... desired the accusation to be rendered up to him again, alleging that he had some more to add thereto. They answered him they would hold what they had, and were ready to receive any other addition when he should please to give it in. The Duke of Norfolk had enough ado to keep his countenance. Mr John Wood winked upon Secretary Cecil, who smiled again upon him.'

Although Bothwell had been in effect rehabilitated by the general assembly in July 1568, there is nothing to indicate that he resumed the 'functions' to which he had been 'restored'. Neither his deprivation in December 1567 nor his subsequent restoration meant that he lost all his revenues or that he subsequently regained them, but the question of the 'third' which had been 'allowed' to him in consideration of his work as an overseer in the diocese must have been raised, and for the years 1567-9 the third of the bishopric of Orkney was listed as 'depending' — that is, in dispute or litigation — between the collector of thirds and the bishop.[87]

A much more drastic change took place in the bishop's position when in 1568 he entered into a contract whereby he in effect exchanged the revenues of the bishopric for those of the abbey of Holyrood, of which Lord Robert Stewart had been in possession as commendator. It is not difficult to see why the bishop agreed to this. One reason for his acceptance of such a bargain may have been his ill-health, of which he still complained (although he survived for another twenty-five years in the less arduous life of a lord of session resident in

Edinburgh). But undoubtedly the principal cause of the bishop's abdication of his see was the determined enmity of the utterly unscrupulous Lord Robert. Bothwell complained that Lord Robert had 'violently intruded himself in his whole living, with bloodshed and hurt of his servants',[88] and this is borne out by record evidence which discloses that some of Lord Robert's followers seized Kirkwall Cathedral by force and murdered some of the bishop's servants.[89]

The bishop was to make over to Lord Robert, in feu, all the lands, mills and fishings of the bishopric not already set in feu and to give him a tack for nineteen years (to be renewed) of the teind sheaves of the lands thus feued to him; the entire revenues of the bishopric, from lands and teinds, were to be set in tack to Robert (which would give him the feu duties of lands already feued to others); when Robert went south on a visit, the bishop was to deliver to him, on the shore of Leith, two chalders of flour and four chalders of meal, with 200 thraves of straw; in Kirkwall Robert was to have the bishop's artillery and munition in his 'castle of the yards'; he was to be bailie and justiciar of the bishop's regality and constable of the castle; the bishop was not to consent to a feu by any Orcadian cleric unless Robert agreed, whereas if Robert obtained such a feu, the bishop was obliged to give his consent; the bishop's rights of patronage were to be transferred to Lord Robert 'if the law will permit' (and we know from later evidence that in general the law did permit). Robert, on his part, was to pay all taxations and dues from the bishopric, to uphold the cathedral, school, castle and yards, to pay the bishop £500 yearly, to cause William Lauder, the bishop's chamberlain, to go to Edinburgh and account for the revenues intromitted with by him from 1567, and he was to put away all malice and hatred he had towards certain persons.[90] This was not in itself much of a bargain for Adam. But the contract says nothing about Holyrood, which was worth between £5000 and £6000 a year. It would therefore appear that the bishop was going to be much in pocket, even allowing for the pension of £1000 which he was obliged to pay Robert from the Holyrood revenues.[91] Robert, of course, was going to recoup himself from what he could wring out of the people in the islands, and the fact that he had entered into such an agreement shows just how much he expected to be able to exploit the bishopric property which he had now acquired.

Adam Bothwell, of course, retained the title of bishop, and in law he still had a certain traditional authority. He did not, however, receive a further commission from the general assembly, and his diocesan duties as an overseer were instead committed to James Annand and Gilbert Foulsie as 'commis..ioners' or 'superintendents'.

The general assembly could not, however, wholly ignore Bothwell, whether as ex-overseer or as present commendator, and in March 1569/70 certain accusations were brought against him:[92]

> Being called to the office of bishopric and promoted to the profit thereof...
> he received the charge of preaching of the evangel, to be also commissioner

in Orkney, which he accepted and executed for a certain space thereafter, until now of late he hath made a simoniacal change of the same with the abbacy of Holyroodhouse, yet still enjoying the name and style of Bishop of the same, contrary to all the laws of God and man made against simony.

He hath demitted the said office and cure into the hands of an unqualified person without consent and licence asked and granted by the assembly, leaving the flock destitute without shepherd ... and hath simpliciter left the office of preaching, giving himself daily to exercise the office of a temporal judge ... and styleth himself with Roman titles, as Reverend Father in God, which pertaineth to no ministers of Christ Jesus.

To the great hurt and defraud of the kirk, he hath all the thirds of the said abbacy ...

That he neither planteth kirks destitute of ministers in either of the said rooms [that is, Orkney and Holyrood], neither sufficiently provideth nor sustaineth the small number planted before his entry ...

All the said kirks, for the most part, wherein Christ's evangel may be preached, are decayed ...

The assembly's attitude is at points instructive: it was clearly accepted that the tenure of a bishopric involved spiritual functions, that bishoprics should be in the hands of persons qualified to perform such functions, that Adam had been a 'shepherd of the flock' and had acted as a commissioner. The accusation of not 'planting kirks' was doubly unfair, because, as we have seen, Bothwell had planted reformed clergy in the diocese of Orkney, while the business of planting ministers in churches appropriated to the abbacy of Holyrood was the business of the superintendent of Lothian and not of the commendator of the abbey.

The bishop's answers to these accusations are also instructive:

It is true that in the 58 year of God, before the reformation of religion, he was, according to the order then observed, provided to the bishopric of Orkney; and when idolatry and superstition were suppressed, he suppressed the same also in his bounds, preached the Word, administered the sacraments, planted ministers in Orkney and Shetland, disponed benefices and gave stipends out of his rents to ministers, exhorters and readers; and when he was a commissioner visited all the kirks of Orkney and Shetland twice, to the hazard of his life in dangerous storms on the seas ... till he was suspended from the exercise of the same commission in 1567, by reason of his infirmity ... at which time he desired some other place to travail in, which was then thought reasonable.

He denied that ever he demitted to my Lord Robert his office, or any part thereof; but that the said Lord Robert violently intruded himself in his whole living, with bloodshed and hurt of his servants ... and then he was constrained, for mere necessity, to take the abbacy of Holyroodhouse.

He denied that he had abandoned absolutely the preaching of the Word, or that he intended to do so, but was to bestow his travails in preaching, as the ability of his body and sickness whereunto he was subject, would suffer or permit. [He thought it good that ministers should be on the Session].

'With pardon and reverence of the assembly, I may declare that I never delighted in such a style as Reverend Father in God'.

That it is true that he had set an assedation of the fruits of the bishopric to the said Lord Robert, for the yearly payment of certain duties contained in his tack ...

That he had no commission to plant or visit since his entry to the abbacy, but if they would give him a conjunct charge with the superintendent of Lothian, he should so travail that they should be satisfied.

He was but of late come to the benefice [of Holyrood], and the most part of these kirks were pulled down by some greedy persons at the first beginning of the reformation.

Whether the bishop's defence proved acceptable to the assembly does not appear. He is not known to have attended any ordinary assemblies after this, though in January 1571/2 he was chosen by the Regent (his uncle-by-marriage, Mar) as a member of a commission to agree to the findings of an extraordinary assembly or 'convention' which prepared a comprehensive scheme for the disposal of the church property.[93] The one ecclesiastical capacity in which he appears in connection with the diocese of Orkney was that of very occasionally receiving presentations to benefices, although the function of giving collation following on presentation should by statute have fallen to the commissioners, and usually did so fall in practice. As he had ceased to exercise functions of oversight in the reformed church, his activities were hardly now a matter for the assembly's attention. His later relations with the assembly amounted usually to nothing more than coexistence in separate spheres, but in July and October 1580, when the assembly had declared the office of bishop contrary to scripture and 'unlawful', and all holders of sees, whatever their ecclesiastical status, were expected to make a formal submission, Adam Bothwell was required to do so.[94] Adam's day-to-day life had become that of a judge and the manager of the revenues of the abbey of Holyrood, but he seems to have been present at every meeting of parliament down to that of 1592 and he sat on the privy council regularly until nearly the end of his life. He must have acquired an experience of public affairs which was unique in an age when few men in prominent positions had as long a life as he had.

During Mary's reign, Adam Bothwell's career had run on lines remarkably parallel to those of Alexander Gordon. Each had been a bishop under the old regime, each had accepted the reformation and worked for it in his diocese, each had become a lord of session. But after Mary's abdication and flight, in the troubles which followed between her supporters and those of her son, James VI, the careers of the two bishops diverged, for, whereas Gordon was a Queen's Man, Bothwell was a King's Man. The fact that each was in some way equivalent to the other was recognised at the time, for on 26 July 1572, when armistice terms were being discussed, the two were appointed to represent their respective parties.[95]

If ecclesiastical affairs caused few 'cummers' in Adam's later years, financial business and consequent litigation proved almost as trying as ever. There seems to have been a good deal of friction over the fulfilment of the terms of the arrangements made with Lord Robert. As late as 1590 Adam was still taking legal action against Robert for failing to carry out his part of the bargain, and there had been a number of lawsuits in the intervening years.[96] Besides, Lord Robert's undertaking that he would make William Lauder, Adam's chamberlain, account to the bishop did not produce an amicable settlement. In March 1568/9 Adam raised an action in the court of session relating that Lauder, as chamberlain of the bishop's property in Shetland, had uplifted the rents, ferms and other revenues of the bishopric from the tenants and occupiers of the lands, churches and other properties pertaining thereto from the chamberlain depute for crops 1561-4 and by himself for 1565-7, but would make no account, reckoning or payment 'bot alluterlie postponis and dyfferis to do the samin without he be compelit'. The record of these proceedings is partly illegible, but it seems that no conclusion was reached at that stage. Then in autumn 1569, when Lauder was setting out for Edinburgh to settle his accounts with the bishop, he was first detained by Lord Robert and then compelled to embark so hastily he had to leave his business papers, and even some of his clothes, behind. Lauder therefore arrived in Edinburgh without his papers, and although he brought witnesses to prove the truth of his story and promised to produce the accounts as soon as he could, he was imprisoned by the bishop in the latter's dwelling place in the abbey of Holyrood, on 9 October 1569. In the prisoner's own words, 'the said reverend father lockit the said Mr William in ane cauld fast house ... quhair wes na fyre nor eisment and swerit be his gret aith that the said Maister William should not be thoilit to cum out of the said place' until he made reckoning, notwithstanding his wanting of his writings and account books. Lauder was in terror that he might be kept in prison for life, and was much affected by 'the wanting of fire, and great cauld' and he appealed to the lords of council. The bishop's attitude appears to have been most unreasonable, but the narrative we have is Lauder's and no doubt there was something to be said on the other side. However, whether under compulsion or under threats, Lauder a few days later (15 October) signed a bond acknowledging that he had intromitted with the bishop's duties in Shetland, consisting of teinds and land-rents, for four years and was owing $306\frac{1}{2}$ angel nobles and 21 'zopindaillis', which he pledged himself to pay.[97] When Adam Bothwell died in 1593, 10,000 merks were still owing to him by the heir of a former chamberlain.[98]

The bishop had another debtor, in the person of the king himself, though this item is tactfully omitted from the list of debts due to him contained in his testament: some time after 1580 the bishop lent the king £500, on security of 'ane greit rubie set in golde'; Adam's son, John, returned the ruby without receiving the £500 and the king was in 1595 graciously pleased to give him a discharge, renouncing 'all actioun and instance that we may have against him as sone and air to his said father'.[99]

There were a number of other loose ends remaining from the complications of the bishopric revenues, which led to a series of lawsuits with Gilbert Balfour[100] and some litigation with William Henderson, the collector of thirds.[101] In 1569, too, Adam had to sue Archibald Ruthven in connection with his pension from the bishopric[102] and was at law with Timothy Cagneoli in connection with the 200 merks the bishop had borrowed from him ten years before.[103] Nor was the commendatorship of Holyrood a bed of roses, for Adam had trouble with the canons, who repeatedly sued him. On the other hand, in May 1569 Adam accused the canons of illegal proceedings: eight of them, he alleged, 'now daylie endis and subscrivis certane takkis of landis and teinds ... impetrat be sundry personis fra his predecessour sen his provision to the said abbacie, and antedaitis the same.'[104] There were 'cummers' over the revenues due to Adam from the abbey, which led to further litigation.[105]

As commendator of Holyrood, Adam had a residence, the 'Commendator's House', adjoining the palace to the north and in front of the entrance to the abbey church, but he may have found it more convenient to live in the house which goes by his name in Byres' Close, just east of the present St Giles Street; part of the structure can still be seen. It was immediately opposite the tolbooth where Adam sat as a member of the Court of Session.[106]

It had in one way and another been a rackety life, which can serve as a commentary on the declaration of the first Book of Discipline that superintendents 'must not be suffered to live as your idle bishops have done heretofore', and it had not been a life of 'canonical ease', to quote another phrase used in a similar context. Adam Bothwell had never, so far as we know, been physically assaulted (though he had had a narrow escape in Kirkwall in 1560), but he had endured the hardships of sixteenth-century travel by land and sea, shipwreck and deprivation of his property, he had suffered at the hands of his kinsmen and co-religionists as well as at those of strangers and ecclesiastical opponents, he had suffered in the capital of Scotland as well as in remote northern islands. 'In journeyings often, in perils of waters, in perils of robbers, in perils by mine own countrymen, in perils by the heathen, in perils in the city, in perils in the wilderness, in perils among false brethren'.

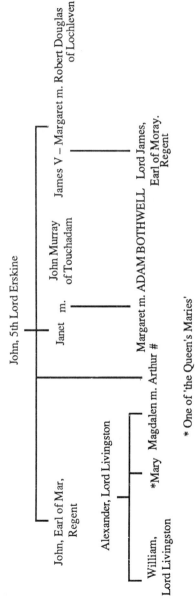

ADAM BOTHWELL'S CONNECTIONS THROUGH MARRIAGE

John, 5th Lord Erskine

James V – Margaret m. Robert Douglas of Lochleven

John Murray of Touchadam

Janet m.

Margaret m. ADAM BOTHWELL   Lord James, Earl of Moray. Regent

John, Earl of Mar, Regent

Alexander, Lord Livingston

William, Lord Livingston

*Mary   Magdalen m. Arthur #

* One of 'the Queen's Maries'
# 'Queen Mary's favourite equerry'

THE BOTHWELL FAMILY AND ITS KINSFOLK

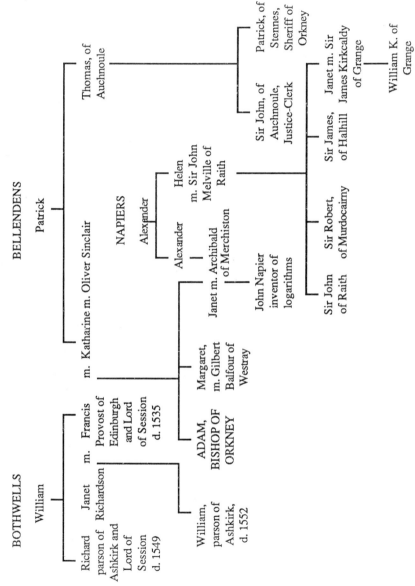

1 *REO,* 363 et seq.; *RMS,* iii, 3102.
2 *RSS,* iv, 916.
3 *CSP Scot.,* i, 102; cf. *REO,* 206; *Public Affairs,* 549; *46th Report of the Deputy Keeper of the Public Records* (1886), App. II, p.63.
4 *Scots Peerage,* s.v. Bothwell, Lord Holyroodhouse; Mark Napier, *Memoirs of John Napier of Merchiston,* (1834), 48 et seq.
5a Knox, i, 28.
5b A & D, xiii, 493.
6 Royal Commission on Ancient Monuments, *Edinburgh Inventory,* 137 and note.
7 *Warrender Papers* (SHS), ii, 396-413; *SHS Miscellany,* i; *Scottish Antiquary,* vii, 132; *Scottish Notes and Queries,* 3rd ser., vi, 198; *Innes Review,* ix, 29, Craven, *History of the Church in Orkney,* ii, 2-3.
8 Duncan Shaw, 'A Conserver of the Renaissance in Scotland', in *Renaissance and Reformation in Scotland* (ed. I.B. Cowan and D. Shaw), 141-69.
9 Napier, op.cit., 234-5.
10 Ibid., 234-42.
11 Knox, ii, 14-16.
12 Reg. of Deeds, ii, 16, 17, 25-6, 75, 135, 253; *RSS,* iv, 1739.
13 *TA,* x, 272, 284; *Protocol Book of Gilbert Grote (SRS),* nos. 182, 184; *RSS,* v, 931.
14 *RSS,* v, 589.
15 Kolsrud, 'Den Norske Kirkes Erkebiskoper og Biskoper', *Diplomatarium Norvegicum,* xvii, sjette hefte, 307.
16 *RMS,* iv, 1668.
17 *RSS,* v, 708, RH 2/1/24, page 101.
18 The calculations of Craven, who was unaware of the date of the provision, are useless. The *anno consecrationis* given in some charters is noted in some later references in this article. Nisbet, in his *Heraldry* (1816), ii, app.p.234, states that Bothwell's election by the chapter of Orkney was confirmed by royal letters patent on 8 October 1562, citing 'Charter under the Great Seal, in the public archives, anno 1562', but no such charter is now to be found.
19 A and D, vii, 118, xv, 294, xviii, 171. I owe these references, and others in this article, to Mr John Ballantyne.
20 Protocol Book of Alexander King, iv, 27 August 1560.
21 A and D, xlii, 230.
23 *TB,* 83-4; A and D, xli, 347 (action relating to Ruthven's pension, 4 May 1569).
24 *Journals of de la Brosse* (SHS), 74-5; *CSP For., Elizabeth,* ii, no.885; *CSP Scot.,* i, no.695.
25 A and D, xx, 166.
26 He left Kirkwall between 20 and 25 April 1561 (Napier, op.cit., 72-4).
27 The letters printed by Napier, op.cit., are now in NLS (MSS. 54.1.6).
28 May 18-24, Kirkwall (A & D, xxii, 85); June 2 (*anno consecrationis* 2), Kirkwall (*RMS,* iv, 1668); June 30 (a.c.l.), *apud capitulum* (Reg. Ho. Miscellaneous Charters, 142), Kirkwall (Mey Papers, 77; Reg. Ho. Calendar of Charters, 1819, 1998); Sept. 20 (a.c.l.), Kirkwall (*REO,* 263); Sept 23, Kirkwall (Reg. Ho. Misc. Charters 47); Oct. 21 (a.c.l.), Kirkwall (Mey Papers, 80); Oct. 22, Kirkwall (Protocol Book of Gilbert Grote [SRS], no.229; Oct 26, 'The Yards' (Napier, 63-4); Dec 1, 'The Yards' (ibid, 64-5); Dec 5 'The Yards' (ibid, 66-7); Jan 19, 'The Yards' (ibid, 65-6); Jan 28 (a.c.2.), 'The Yards' (Craven, ii, 10); Feb 5, Kirkwall (Napier, 68-70); Feb 16, Kirkwall (Reg. of Deeds, iv, 230); March 25, 'Mons Bellus' (i.e. Birsay) (Napier 70-71); April 12 (a.c.2.), Kirkwall (*RMS,* v, 2265; *REO,* 342-3).
29 Napier, 63, 73.
30 Ibid., 63-4.
31 Napier, 65.
32 Knox, i, 97, 219.
33 Napier, 68.
34 Mey Papers, 78; cf. Storer Clouston, *History of Orkney,* 296-7.

35 Napier, 68.
36 *CSP Scot.*, i, 967.
37 Napier, 71; *REO*, 342-4.
38 Napier, 72-6.
39 John Lesley, *History* (ed T. Thomson), 284.
40 Napier, 76-7.
41 A and D, lv, 226 (where he is said to have been provided to his benefices by Bishop Reid); *Protocol Book of Gilbert Grote*, No.164; Craven, 10; *REO* 269, 342; *TB*, 93, 151, 204-5; *Register of Ministers etc, 1567.*
42 Calderwood, iii, 303; cf *BUK*, i, 35.
43a *REO*, 341; *TB*, 205; Reg of Stipends, 1574, 1576; p.34
43b *Yester Writs* (SRS), no.682.
44 Conclusive evidence that a man was serving in the reformed church comes when his third was formally allowed to him on that account; but when the third was not paid in 1561 and the man subsequently appears as a minister or reader the presumption is that he had been so acting in 1561 — as indeed is suggested by the bishop's own case (p.31 above).
45 Mey Papers, 77, 80; Craven, 10; *TB* 93, 124, 151, 204, *RSS*, v, 3308.
46a *St Andrews Records* (SHS), 239; Mey Papers, 80; *REO*, 288, 342, *TB*, 144, 205.
46b *Reg. Colleg. de Glasgow*, 231; a William Lauder matriculated at St Andrews in 1537 with Francis Bothwell, but another matriculated there in 1542 and the latter is more likely to have become the bishop's associate.
46c Mey Papers, 80; *REO*, 263; *TB*, 149, 204; *RSS*, v, 3174; Reg Pres., ii, 130.
47a *Essays in Shetland History*, 154.
47b *BUK*, i, 26; *TB*, x, note.
48 *TB*, 115, 152; the passages are quoted from the MS.
49 *BUK*, i, 32.
50 Ibid., 35, 38-45, 52 *et seq.*, 60, 77, 90.
51 Ibid., 35; Edin. Comm. A & D (CC8/2/1), 31 March 1565.
52 Mey Papers, 93 (Dunbeath in Caithness, 26 June 1562 [a.c.6 (sic)]; Reg. No. Misc. Charters, 114 (Kirkwall, 12 July 1563); ibid., 20 (*Apud Capitulum*, 16 Oct 1564 [a.c.6.]); Mey Papers, 165 (Kirkwall, 18 Oct 1564); *REO*, 285 (Kirkwall, 26 Aug 1566).
53 After leaving Orkney in April 1561 he went to France, returning in August to Edinburgh, where he is found in September, February and June following (Reg of Deeds, iv, 342, v, 159; A and D, xxxi, 64). He was in Edinburgh on 30 April and 28 June, 1563 (Reg Pres, ii, 35, 130) and again in December 1563 (*BUK*, i, 38-45), January and March 1564 (Books of Sederunt, ii, 86; Reg. Ho. Charters, 1935; Craven, 28; Mey Papers, 104). From that point his periods of residence in Edinburgh can be followed more fully from the Records of the Court of Session, of which he was now a judge.
54 *BUK*, i, 112.
55 Ibid., 165.
56 Ibid., 52.
57 E.g., *RSS*, v, 2663, 2833; vi, 595, 597, 599; vii, 2350; RSS (MS), 52.76v; Craven 29; Goudie, *Antiquities of Shetland* 147.
58 E.g., Craven, 29.
59 Craven, 29.
60 *Essays in Shetland History*, 156-7.
61 *BUK*, i, 112.
62 Justiciary Court Books of Adjournal, xiii, 63, 67.
63 Calderwood, iv, 163; Wodrow Soc., *Miscellany*, i, 417.
64 Pitcairn, *Criminal Trials*, I, i, 413*; Justiciary Court Records (JCI), 9 Dec 1561, 23 Apr 1562, 13 May 1562.

65 A & D, xxiv, 375; xxv, 217, 249; xxvii, 278-9; xxxi, 62-3, 88, 180; xxxv, 20; xxxvi, 413; Reg. of Deeds v. 159; Reg. of Deeds, Warrants (RD/11/3), 3 June 1564; Protocol Book of James Nicolson, abstract (RH 2/1/19), p.112.
70 A & D, xxi, 67, 253.
71 Ibid., xxii, 85.
72 Ibid., xxxi, 67, 206, 278, 384.
75 Craven, 25.
76 A and D, xxx, 321; xxxi, 58.
77 A and D, xxxi, 64.
78 A & D, xxxi, 88; *RMS*, iv, 1710.
79a A & D, xxxi, 140. The 'Register of Orknay' may have been a register of charters granted by the bishops.
79b TB, xxvii-xxviii; *RPC*, i, 487-8; *RSS*, v, p, xiv.
80 Napier, *op.cit.*, 116-7; Sir James Melville, *Memoirs*, 179; Hay Fleming, *Mary Queen of Scots*, 455.
81 Donaldson, *The First Trial of Mary, Queen of Scots*, 150.
82 Keith, ii, 710, 722.
83· Laing's *Knox*, vi, 556; NLS, Wodrow MSS, 8vo vol.6 no.4; *RPC*, i, 543; McCrie, *Knox* (1874), 259.
84 *TB*, 191; Collector's Account for 1579 (E/45/13).
85 *BUK*, i, 112, 114.
86 Ibid., 131.
87 *TB.*, 67-9.
88 *BUK*, i, 165.
89 *RSS*, vi, 306, 423, 504.
90 A & D, xlii, 340.
91 *RSS*, vi, 506.
92 *BUK*, i, 162-3 (given in somewhat modernised language).
93 Calderwood, iii, 170.
94 Ibid., 465, 474-5.
95 Richard Bannatyne, *Memorials* (Bannatyne Club), 239.
96 RSS, lxii, 79; lxiii, 89; A & D, xliv, 108.
97 A & D, xliii, 341; *Protocol Book of Gilbert Grote*, no.318; *Court Book of The Burgh of Canongate and Regality and Barony of Broughton* (Marguerite Wood, 1937) 87; Craven, 25-6.
98 Edinburgh Tests, 24 December 1608.
99 Napier, 277-8.
100 A & D, xlv, 18, 161; xlvi, 169, 296, 318; liii, 193; lvi, 132, 392.
101 Ibid., xlvii, 11.
102 Ibid., xli, 347.
103 Ibid., xlii, 230.
104 Ibid., xli, 365; xlvi, 53.
105 Ibid., xli, 331, 349, 365, 372; xlii, 250, 360, 365, 369, 528; xliii, 340; xliv, 152, 165; xlv, 40, 231; xlvi, 169, 216.
106 Mr John Ballantyne has drawn my attention to papers relating to this property in Register of Deeds (B 22/8/8), fos. 308-19, 330-3, 405-7.

ROBERT STEWART, BISHOP OF CAITHNESS

As a brother of Matthew Stewart, fourth Earl of Lennox, Robert Stewart was a typical aristocratic bishop of the period, taking his place alongside brothers of the Earls of Huntly who were bishops of Aberdeen and Galloway, a brother of the Earl of Bothwell who was bishop of Moray, and brothers or at any rate half-brothers of the Earl of Arran who were archbishop of St Andrews and bishop of Argyll. But Robert Stewart was in some respects of even higher social standing than those contemporaries of his. By the marriage of his brother, Earl Matthew, to Margaret Douglas, daughter of Margaret Tudor and granddaughter of Henry VII, Bishop Robert stood close to the English royal family; and by the marriage of his nephew, Lord Darnley, to Queen Mary — a marriage which made Darnley 'Henry, King of Scots' — he stood even closer to the Scottish royal line. Indeed, had James VI died before reaching the age of twenty, only one or (briefly) two frail lives would have stood between the bishop and the possibility of his becoming Robert IV, king of Scots.

Robert had been born apparently in 1523 and while still in his youth was appointed to the provostry of the collegiate church of Dumbarton, which was a Lennox foundation. As early as April 1539 he seems to have been earmarked for the bishopric of Caithness, for at that point he was nominated by the crown on a premature report of the bishop's death. When the bishop — the second of two Andrew Stewarts who held the see in succession — did actually die, little time was lost in making a fresh nomination of this third Stewart, Robert, on 8 September 1541, and he was provided on 27 January 1541/2.[1] He had received the first tonsure, indicating that he was destined for a clerical career, but at the age of nineteen he could not be a priest or deacon, let alone a bishop, and he was therefore provided only as administrator, which at this stage presumably meant nothing more than administrator of the revenues, in other words, ability to grant charters and tacks. He granted a feu charter to John Gray, of lands in Culmalye, on 2 March 1543/4.[2] The appointment as administrator was to last until his twenty-seventh year, when he was to have full title. As he was not consecrated, he was generally styled 'postulate' (indicating that there was some 'defect', in his case age), 'elect', or 'elect confirmed', but he derived emoluments from the see from the date of his provision for the rest of his days.

It was no plum that fell into Robert's hands. According to the figures given in the Books of Assumption and the Accounts of the Collectors of Thirds[3] the revenues amounted to only £1284 and six dozen geese. This was the lowest figure recorded for any see in Scotland, slightly behind Orkney and Galloway

and a little more behind Dunblane. St Andrews, by comparison, was worth
£6430 and Dunkeld £4534. The rather low figure for Caithness may be suspect,
since only money is mentioned — apart from the geese — whereas in some
other sees the revenues in victual far exceeded in value the amount due in
money and indeed the rental of Caithness does say, after the money and the
geese, 'all uther thingis omittit'. It must also be remembered that the
Assumption of Thirds did not extend to Argyll and the Isles, which may well
have been the poorest sees of all. However, with all qualifications, Caithness
was not a plum.

It was even less of a plum when important deductions were made, for Robert
did not obtain all the revenues of the see. As was usual in that period, the
appointment to the see was accompanied by grants of pensions: in this case 500
merks went to a natural son of the Earl of Moray (himself a natural son of James
IV), 200 merks to George Lesley, clerk of St Andrews diocese, and 40 merks to
George Busco, also clerk of St Andrews diocese. These pensions amounted to
740 merks or £500, which was more than a third of the total revenues.[4]

Within a year of Robert Stewart's appointment to the see, James V was dead
and the stirring events which followed involved the new bishop. His brother
Earl Matthew came back from France, initially as a French agent, to contest
the rights of James, Earl of Arran, who had been appointed Governor, and
when Arran made his remarkable *volte face* which ended the 'godly fit' in which
he had favoured an English alliance and the reformed cause, Lennox went over
to the English side and became an agent of Henry VIII. On 17 May 1543, at
Carlisle, the bishop signed a contract whereby Lennox and that conspicuous
friend to reform, the Earl of Glencairn, undertook to aid Henry, who on his
part agreed that Lennox should marry Margaret Douglas and become
Governor of Scotland; Robert was to remain in England as a hostage while
Lennox engaged in military operations in the south-west of Scotland.[5]

Lennox had little success, had to withdraw to England, and in his absence
was forfeited for treason on 9 October 1545. The proceedings against his
brother the bishop were more protracted. As early as 12 December 1544 the
Scottish government asked the pope to summon Robert Stewart for his
misdeeds and give the see of Caithness to Alexander Gordon, brother of the
Earl of Huntly.[6] Gordon, under the style 'postulate of Caithness', seems to have
gained at least partial possession of the revenues and did not resign his claim
until 1548. But in 1545, when Lennox was forfeited, his brother the bishop, who
in any event obtained a crown remission on 6 August,[7] escaped forfeiture
because, as a clerk, he was repledged to the spiritual authority.[8] That
authority, in the person of Cardinal Beaton, who of course was on the French
and conservative side, sequestrated Robert's revenues in the hands of the
principales personae — the chief dignitaries — of the cathedral chapter, on the
ground not only of his political dealings with Henry, which made him guilty of
treason at a time of war between the two countries, but also on the ground of his

association with Henry's schismatic subjects.[9] If the cardinal was more than merely conventionally shocked by the guilt of schism, one wonders how he reacted to Robert Stewart's next ploy. On 24 March 1545/6 he was presented by the schismatic English king to a prebend of Canterbury in the now schismatic Church of England.[10] According to the statutes of the cathedral, the holder of this prebend ought to have been a priest, but the statutes were not always observed. In 1544 it had been repeated that Robert had not yet progressed beyond the first tonsure,[11] and he was not yet quite of age for priest's orders when he obtained his prebend. He did not hold it long, for he had resigned it by 9 May 1548, when a successor was appointed.[12] He did not even remain long in England, for on 11 April 1546, less than three weeks after his appointment to the prebend, he was despatched to Scotland and he landed at Dumbarton on 27 May.[13] He was still in Scotland in September.[14]

It was clearly his business to make his peace with the Scottish government and with his rival, Alexander Gordon. On 16 July 1546 he had submitted to the governor and the crown. Alexander was to enjoy the bishopric, and the provostry of Dumbarton (which Robert had resigned)[15] was to be given to anyone nominated by the governor. Robert, however, was to have 'samekle rent be yeir as he had at his departing furth of Scotland', which implied a compromise in financial terms.[16] Two more years passed before there was a full settlement.[17] Then it was agreed that Gordon was to have not the bishopric but a pension of 500 merks from its revenues. This deduction, added to the pensions reserved on Robert's appointment, left him with only about a third of the episcopal revenues.

From 1546 the bishop was certainly a good deal in Scotland and may even have been there with little intermission. After that formal submission in person to the governor in July 1546 we know that he was in Scotland in September, and we know again that he was before the council in 1548. In 1549 he was at Dornoch, where an edict under his signature was issued in July.[18] In September 1550 he went with Mary of Guise to France. At that point the queen dowager was accompanied by a group of notables, apparently selected because they were inclined to the cause of reform, so that they could be subjected to French influence and exposed to French offers: the journey has been called a 'brainwashing expedition'. It would appear, however, that in the case of Robert Stewart the initiative came from him, to the extent at least that he had learned of the proposed expedition and asked if he could join it, for on 13 June 1550 he had written to the dowager that he had 'hard that your grace, God willing, purpoisis in France and gif it plesit your grace I wald pas thair to the sculis and to do sik service as your grace will charge me to, swa that I had my Lord Governor licence to depart'.[19] Robert duly received the governor's licence and set out for France, where he remained until at least October 1551.[20] He compeared before the lords of council in Edinburgh on 4 July 1554 and was in Scotland in 1555. A charter by him was dated at Dornoch on 26 March 1557;

he granted a precept of sasine under his seal on 18 January 1558/9; he granted a tack at Dornoch on 16 August and a charter there on 14 September 1560.[21]

The Bishop was clearly in close touch with the course of events in Scotland, but the only evidence, and it is slight, of his possible attitude comes from a curious quarter. One John Elder, who is best known as an earnest propagandist on behalf of Henry VIII in 1543 — which meant he was an ally of the Lennoxes — was a native of Caithness, as he himself says.[22] In 1555 a letter by Elder to 'the right reverend and his very especial good lord Robert Stuard, bishop of Caithness and provost of Dumbarton College in Scotland', was published in London. It achieved some note because of the account it gives of the marriage of Mary Tudor to Philip of Spain and the reception of Cardinal Pole in England. By this time Elder had accommodated himself to the new ecclesiastical climate in England and went so far as to protest that he had never had association with heretics.[23] Perhaps the only thing we can deduce from the letter is that Elder may have been in the habit of keeping the bishop informed about events in England, but he may have had hopes of encouraging Robert to follow his example and relapse into popery.

Whatever else Robert Stewart may have been doing in the 1540s and 1550s, it is abundantly clear that he was managing, or perhaps more accurately mismanaging, the episcopal revenues — another aspect of what we may call the 'tulchan' principle. There are many signs that there had been heavy pressure towards the secularisation of church property in Caithness. Robert's absence in the course of his association with Lennox's proceedings in 1543-4 had given acquisitive local magnates opportunities for spoliation. In 1544 the Earl of Caithness and Donald Mackay of Farr seized the lands and rents of the bishopric and occupied the castles of Skibo and Scrabster. They said that they had done this in Robert's name but on his return they refused to disgorge their gains until they were reduced to submission and the bishop repossessed through the intervention of the Earls of Sutherland and Huntly (who were cousins).[24] No doubt Sutherland was no altruist and felt that he had earned the bishop's gratitude, which, as we shall see, was forthcoming in ample form.

Next, it did the property no good to be the subject of contention — physical contention — between Alexander Gordon, the claimant to the see, and Robert's supporters. On 30 March 1548, when Gordon was on the point of renouncing his claim, Robert, elect of Caithness, John Matheson, the chancellor, Hercules Barclay, parson of Canisbay, and three others, found surety to underlie the law on 30 April for taking and detaining from Alexander Gordon, postulate of Caithness, the house and place of Scrabster, and for seizing the fruits of the bishopric.[25] In 1549 Articles by the bishop accused the Earl of Caithness of various excesses, including sacrilegious violence against clergy and spoliation of churches, in the case of Farr to the extent that the sacraments could not be ministered there.[26]

However, once Robert was both *de jure* and *de facto* in the saddle, in 1549, he granted a feu charter to the Earl of Caithness of several lands in the north-east of the diocese, including the lands of Mey and the island of Stroma.[27] in 1553 he made the Earl of Sutherland heritable bailie of the bishopric and in 1557 granted to his countess extensive lands which surely constituted a very large part of the temporality and included even the palace of Dornoch.[28] He granted the earl more lands in 1559 and 1560.

In these proceedings we see the significance of Robert's appointment as administrator, which gave him power over the episcopal property. Normally, during a vacancy in a see the episcopal temporality fell to the crown and was made over to the new bishop only after he was consecrated, but Robert's charters show that he was invested with the temporality although he was never consecrated. However, the crown was in the habit of granting the temporality of a vacant see to some individual or other, and there was nothing to hinder such a grant being made to a bishop-elect. Not only so, but the crown was showing some inclination, in the years before 1560, to revive its claim to the spirituality as well, and there are instances in religious houses where the crown granted temporality and spirituality alike, in anticipation of provision. If this happened with Caithness, everything falls into place. The pope granted Robert the title, the crown granted him the substance.

The diocese of Caithness, where Robert Stewart was firmly established several years before the conventional date of the Scottish reformation, fell into two parts which could hardly have been more different one from the other. There was Caithness proper, the ness or peninsula of the ancient province of Cat, stretching out to the north-east, with its low, indeed flat, landscape, its fertile, corn-growing fields, even today still visibly part of the northern region of Scotland with its strong Scandinavian heritage. I sometimes think, travelling north to Thurso, that one reaches Orkney not on crossing the Pentland Firth but before that, on emerging from the mountainous wastes of Sutherland and descending to the farmsteads of the Caithness plains. In the sixteenth century there may have been audible as well as visual signs of the affinity of Caithness with the north, for the Norse speech was probably not yet extinct.[29] The other main part of the diocese, roughly the later county of Sutherland, had a totally different character. There was a tenuous fringe of fertile land around Dornoch, where the cathedral lay on the very boundary of the diocese, forming a nexus with Fortrose cathedral in fertile Easter Ross and Elgin cathedral in the even more fertile Laich of Moray. And narrow ribbons of comparative fertility extended along riversides up some of the straths. But the mass of Sutherland was and always has been a synonym for desolation, stretching as it does through interminable inland wastes to the stark and bare, almost lunar, landscape of the west and north-west. The area of Caithness is only a third of that of Sutherland, but in 1755 Caithness had a slightly larger population than its larger but barren neighbour. Ecclesiastically viewed, of the 23 parishes in the diocese of

Caithness $9\frac{1}{2}$ were in little Caithness while $13\frac{1}{2}$ straggled over the vast wilderness of Sutherland. (The halves are explained by the parish of Reay, which straddled the county boundary.) Wild country meant wild men, and there is plenty of evidence of the rapacity and violence of the Mackays on the north coast and the Earl of Sutherland in the south; but even the Caithness Sinclairs were not always models of civility.

Yet, with all the geographical and social diversity, there was a certain unity or uniformity about the ecclesiastical pattern, to the extent at least that every parish in the diocese was appropriated and the appropriation was in every case to a diocesan or cathedral unit — the bishop's *mensa*, a dignitary or canon, or the chapter in common. There was not a religious house in the diocese, but the parish of Kildonan had originally been given to the abbey of Scone, which retained rights in the prebend which was created later. The parishes were all served by vicars, with very small stipends.

At precisely what date the bishop began to take a hand in organising the reformed church in his diocese is not quite clear. We do know that he was at Dornoch on 16 August 1560 and at Scrabster on 24 February 1561[30] and it is not impossible that he then appointed the first members of the reformed ministry, though so far as we can see there were only one or two at that stage. His commitment to the reformation cannot have been in any doubt in view of his record over most of the last two decades, and it was hardly surprising that at the end of 1561, when he was in Edinburgh, the English ambassador reported that he 'comes daily to the sermon and is reputed honest enough'.[31] Nor does there seem to have been any difficulty about his acceptance into the ministry of the reformed church, whatever precise ecclesiastical status he had held under the unreformed dispensation. He was acknowledged a 'minister professor of the true religion'.[32] Possibly, as in Orkney and Galloway, it was just taken for granted that the bishop would conduct the administration, but the acceptance of Robert Stewart as an official of the reformed church does raise certain questions not applicable in the cases of Gordon and Bothwell. The fact that Stewart had not been consecrated in the traditional manner would not in itself be an obstacle in the eyes of at least some reformers, who expressly set themselves against the conventional idea of a tactual succession, which they rejected on the ground that 'the miracle is now ceased'. But the question remained how far the bishop had been previously involved in ecclesiastical administration, in other words how the diocese had been managed during the long period when there had not been a consecrated bishop. Normally, in such circumstances the running of the diocese would be in the hands of the dean, or possibly the chantor, as vicar general and president of the chapter. The sacramental functions of a bishop in ordination and confirmation would not be carried out, but this did not mean that there was no supply of priests, as men ordained by bishops of other dioceses could be instituted to charges in Caithness by the vicar general, while confirmation would not be much missed, for all the indications are that it was only intermittently administered at the best of times. The judicial business of the see — the work of the ecclesiastical courts — would go on without any difficulty, and there is ample evidence of the operation in the 1550s of a commissary general for the whole diocese and a commissary substitute with an 'office' — the word is used — at Thurso.[33] So far as the supervision of the clergy was concerned, the archdeacon would act irrespective of the existence of a bishop.

It would appear that so far as admission to benefices was concerned the machinery usual during vacances operated: that is, presentations were directed to the vicars general, who gave collation; there are certainly several examples of this in the 1540s.[34] However, in 1551, when the bishop was in France with the dowager, James Brady, the archdeacon, was described as *his* vicar general during his absence, which suggests that the bishop was in some way associated with the administration of the diocese. All in all, it is not difficult to see why it seemed reasonable enough to accept Stewart as the 'overseer' of the diocese in the interests of the reformed church in 1561. Apparently he did not, like Gordon and Bothwell, at once enjoy remission of his third in return for his labours, but later, as we shall see, his third was remitted on special conditions.

There are exceptional difficulties in tracing the expansion of the reformed ministry in Caithness, because there are no Accounts of Sub-collectors of Thirds extant for that area until so late as 1569 and our information is therefore largely a blank between the Accounts of the Collector General in 1561 and 1562 and the Register of Ministers which begins in 1567. The Accounts of the Collector General for 1561 and 1562 show very little in the way of a reformed ministry in the diocese. In both years Mr Thomas Brady was allowed the third of his pension from the archdeaconry (which was financed from the parishes of Bower and Watten) as part of his stipend as exhorter as Bower, and Walter Innes was allowed the third of his vicarage of Thurso as minister there. It may be significant that these two conformers were neighbours in adjoining parishes — Thurso, Bower and Watten — in the most civilised part of the diocese, I mean Caithness proper. But they were not the only men in the reformed ministry: these Accounts of the Collectors General give only lump sums for stipends for each area, without giving names, and to make matters worse the area for which such figures are given is the whole of 'Inverness-shire', including Ross and modern Inverness-shire as well as Sutherland and Caithness. The total for stipends for this huge area was only £380 in 1561 and rose to £650 in 1562, and no doubt some of this expansion was in the diocese of Caithness. There can be little doubt that some of the men who are not named as ministers, readers and exhorters until later were already there in 1561 or 1562, like sir James Scott, an ex-priest, who turns up as minister of Skinnet in 1566, and perhaps sir Alexander Mearns, who had been vicar of Wick in 1548 and certainly became reader there at a later date. Curiously enough, these men too were in parishes in Caithness proper, where it would appear that the reformation was making more headway than elsewhere in the diocese.

If progress generally throughout the diocese was slow the reason was almost certainly financial: the acquisitive local lords and lairds ensured that funds which should have been available for the support of the reformed ministry were simply not there. In 1561 the Earl of Sutherland was at the horn for the thirds of the vicarage of Culmallie, the vicarage of Kildonan, the chantory and part of the third of the bishopric; Y McKy of Far for another part of the third of the bishopric and part of the third of the parsonage and vicarage of Farr; and Angus McKilyemoir and Tormount McKennymoir for the third of the vicarage of Durness. The Account for 1562 presents an even more gloomy picture, for in addition to those thirds which had not been recovered there was another hunk of the bishopric in the hands of the chamberlain of the countess of Sutherland, a third of the vicarage of Wick in the hands of an individual styled 'factor or at the least intromitter', which suggests some doubt about his legal status, and a third of the parsonage and vicarage of Assynt in the hands of Neil Angusson in Assynt.

There was little sign of improvement in financial resources down to 1572. Durness, Assynt, Farr, Culmallie and Wick were still apparently yielding nothing, and there were problems with Canisbay, Latheron, Loth and Reay. Conditions were extremely disturbed: there was a feud between the Mackays and the Murrays, and Mackay of Strathnaver and the Earl of Caithness raided Skibo and burned Dornoch in 1566-7. And yet, once we emerge into the light of day with the Register of Ministers (from 1567) and the Sub-Collectors' Accounts (from 1569) we find that, however and whenever the situation of a reformed ministry had improved, improved it assuredly had. There were now five ministers, nine exhorters and eight readers, a total of 22, which was as nearly as possible one officiant for each of the 23 parishes in the diocese. In 1574, after there had been a general reorganisation and rationalisation throughout the whole kingdom, the Caithness parishes were systematically arranged in nine groups, each intended to have a minister with the oversight of two or three readers. Assynt was vacant, but the total strength was eight ministers and 16 readers. Stipends for Caithness alone were now over £800.

The bishop was involved in two ways. His position had been regularised, if not strengthened, by decisions of the general assembly. Its records are gravely defective, and it is peculiarly reckless to advance any argument from silence. All we can say is that Robert Stewart is first mentioned in June 1563, in a context which suggests that he was already active — and indeed he clearly must have been, in view of the beginnings of the reformed ministry. The assembly at that point commissioned Donald Monro, archdeacon of the Isles, who might have been thought to have more than enough to do already as commissioner of the diocese of Ross, 'to assist the bishop of Caithness in preaching of the gospel and planting of kirks'. The bishop himself, with his fellow conformers of Orkney and Galloway, received a commission at that time, but whether it was the first such commission cannot be determined.[35] In July 1568 Robert again received a commission for a year,[36] and in 1571, when he was designated 'head commissioner' of the diocese, additional manpower was requested, and the assembly, 'not finding a man fit, for the present, for such a charge, in that country', asked John Gray of Fordell to continue 'in his supporting of the said diocese, with the assistance of the bishop thereof, head commissioner of the same' — a curious turn of phrase, which suggests bad drafting.[37] It seems reasonable to conclude that the bishop was fairly steadily engaged in his diocese over these years, in the interests of the reformed church, and there is certainly evidence that he was quite often present within the bounds. He was at Skibo on 15 February 1565/6,[38] at Scrabster on 1 June 1566,[39] at Dornoch on 26 August 1566[40] and was 'resident in Caithness' when Dornoch was burned in 1567.[41] Stewart was not only appointing ministers, but also giving collation to benefices in his capacity as a reformed bishop (for superintendents and commissioners had as yet no such power) e.g.: collation of the deanery to Gavin Borthwick, 2 June 1566.[42] His position in this respect received statutory basis in 1567, when commissioners as well as superintendents were authorised to receive presentations and give collation.[43]

The other way in which the bishop was involved in the expansion of the reformed ministry was financial. The general assembly of July 1568, when it renewed his commission, decided that for his stipend he should have 'the whole third of the bishopric remitted, providing that he sustain ministers in his own kirks therefrom'. It was added that 'the rest of the ministers of the diocese' were 'to be sustained upon the rest of the thirds according to their stipends already modified.[44] This idea was not novel, because it had a little earlier been alleged that 'the thirds of Caithness bishopric' were to be paid by the bishop 'to his ministers of his own kirks'.[45] This scheme clearly operated, because the Accounts of the Sub-Collectors for 1569-72 state that the third of the bishopric of Caithness was to remain with the bishop for the support of ministers in his churches of Durness, Reay, Thurso, Wick, Latheron, Loth and Culmallie and that he was also to have the thirds of the vicarages of Thurso and Reay for the support of readers there.[46] The third of the bishopric was remitted to the bishop so late as 1579,[47] but now without any conditions attached.

A change in the bishop's personal circumstances had come about when, on 9 October 1570, he had been appointed commendator of St Andrews priory, in succession to the Regent Moray, who had been murdered in January. This must for one thing have transformed Robert's financial position, for that house had been reckoned in 1561 to be worth some £12,500, and it meant that he had residential quarters in the precincts. There he appears to have settled, for the many charters, tacks and grants of pensions which he issued were from that point dated (when he know the dates) at St Andrews. He probably found it congenial enough to live in the university city. It was, for one thing, a good deal more comfortable than travelling through a northern diocese. Secondly, it suited his intellectual interests, if we can judge them from the books he presented to his grand-nephew, the young James VI.[48] There were Greek and Latin classics, some of them in French translations, a Greek New Testament, the works of a range of reformers — Bullinger, Calvin, Erasmus, Melanchthon — and a book called 'The Perfect Pathway to Salvation'. It is always risky to judge a man from his books, and it might be more risky to judge a man from the books he gives away to a young nephew. If we can make an assessment, it can be said that the volumes speak of wide cultural interests rather than any profound scholarship. At the same time, it must be remembered that Robert Stewart was considered a suitable person for membership of a commission to visit the universities of St Andrews and Glasgow in 1578. But the east coast town, besides providing comfortable quarters and intelligent company, had a third appeal, for Robert was a golfer.

His happiness at St Andrews might have been greater or more enduring had Andrew Melville not become principal there in 1580. This new broom seems, according to his admiring nephew, James, to have made trouble all round. He accused the commendator of failing to appoint a minister for the town and pocketing the vacant stipend. James Melville paints a picture of 'the prior and his gentlemen-pensioners' enjoying themselves with golf, archery, good cheer and so forth.[49] It almost suggests that Robert was keeping a kind of court of men whom he was maintaining on the pensions he granted from the priory, and this may have had some truth in it. It appears that some of the prior's domestic staff, if not his pensioners, got their names if not into the Sunday papers at any rate into the pages of the Register of the local Kirk Session.[50]

While the bishop's work in the diocese had clearly been associated with a considerable expansion of the reformed ministry, it is not clear whether he had been very successful in persuading the clergy who were in office in 1560 to accept office under the new dispensation. It is hard to say much on this, as we are in the dark about the incumbents of so many of the parishes in 1560. As it is, we can point only to Thomas Brady, vicar of Watten, who became reader there; Walter Innes, vicar of Thurso and minister there; Alexander Mearns, who was vicar of Wick in 1548 and presumably the man who appears as reader there in 1576; Robert Ferne, curate at Golspie in 1546 and exhorter there 1569-72. Donald Reid, vicar of Kildonand in 1530, is rather unlikely to be the Donald Reid who was reader at Farr in 1567. James Scott, who was reader or minister at Halkirk and Skinnet in 1566, is styled 'sir James', so presumably was an ex-priest. It should be added that reluctance to serve in the reformed church did not imply any refusal to accept its doctrines, for sir Malcolm Reid, vicar of Reay, had married by the time he died about 1566. At a later stage, as will appear below, the bishop was credited with making sure that the men appointed to benefices after the reformation were qualified to serve in the ministry and we find the following: Alexander Barclay, minister, appointed treasurer, 1579; Archibald Davidson, minister, parson and vicar of Farr 1572;

John Dunnett, minister, parson and vicar of Canisbay 1577; William Gray, exhorter, treasurer in 1580; John Mossman, reader, vicar of Halkirk and Skinnet 1579; Andrew Philp, minister at Wick 1567-72, appointed vicar of Wick 1574; Alexander Urquhart, minister, parson and vicar of Olrig 1573; John Watson or Wobstar, minister, appointed to Canisbay 1572.

Shortly after Robert had been appointed to St Andrews priory there was a change which altered his position in the reformed church, when in 1572 bishops were formally accepted as part of its system. He was no longer merely a relic of the old regime, styled 'elect confirmed', but 'ane reverend fader in God, Robert, bishop of Caithness'. He was also, as prior, dean of the reformed chapter of the see of St Andrews. He was commissioned to take part in the consecrations of John Douglas to St Andrews, George Douglas to Moray and Patrick Adamson to St Andrews.[51] He certainly officiated at Douglas's consecration, an event which provided Bishop Keith with one of those clever debating points for which he had some talent. He wrote: 'though there be no ground to think that this person was ever duly, and according to the constant invariable usage of the primitive Catholic Church, vested with any sacred character, yet it is a little diverting to observe how the men at the helm of public affairs in those days grant commission to him to assist in the consecration of other men to the sacred office of bishops.'[52]

Now that he was fully integrated as a bishop into the reformed church, presentations could be directed to Stewart in that capacity, and they were so directed.[53] In one of these presentations he was designated 'bishop and superintendent', but it is quite possible that after he settled at St Andrews in or about 1571 Caithness never saw him again and he ceased to take part in person in the work of the church there. In 1574 Robert Graham was named as commissioner of Caithness, with a salary of £100. It may be that all that Stewart continued to do was to give collation to presentees, but he had a reputation for using this power in the interests of the reformed church. In 1582 he received a testimonial to the effect that he was 'verray ardent and zelus and movit of conscience that all benefices gret and small within the boundis of the diocy of Caithness, quhen evir thai sal happin to vaik ... sall be gevin, grantit and disponit to sic personis qualifiit baith in literature and maneris, quhilkis sal be fund abill to teiche and preiche the evangill ... and minister the sacramentis', and on this ground rights of presentation were transferred to him.[54] He seems to have deserved this testimonial, because most of the men presented to benefices in the diocese in the 1570s had in fact been ministers, or occasionally exhorters or readers — though whether the figure was higher in Caithness than elsewhere it might be hard to determine. He used the power to present (as distinct from merely giving collation) in appointing Donald Logan to the chantory on 17 July 1584.[55]

Meantime the bishop's position had changed yet again. Charles Stewart, Earl of Lennox, Darnley's brother, had died in 1576, leaving only an infant daughter Arabella, and the earldom passed to Bishop Robert as heir male. When his nephew Esmé Stewart came on the scene, and the infatuated king decided that he should have the earldom of Lennox, the bishop was prevailed on to accept the earldom of March instead. Bishop of Caithness, Commendator of St Andrews, Earl of Lennox, Earl of March — it is perhaps hardly surprising that some writers have become confused. But I see no excuse for a recent reference to 'Queen Mary's Catholic half-brother Robert Stewart, seventh Earl of Lennox', where the error was compounded with the combination of Robert Stewart, Earl of Orkney, and Esmé Stewart, Earl of Lennox, as well as the genuine bishop-commendator-earl.[56] Esmé provided the 'Catholic' element.

It was debatable whether the succession to the throne, failing James VI, would pass to the Hamiltons or the Lennoxes — so debatable that a contemporary remarked that the question would put many men on horseback before it was settled.[57] But, granted that the Lennox claim was the better, then, after Arabella, who might have been thought disqualified as an English subject, Bishop Robert was heir presumptive. Very likely it was because of his proximity to the throne after the death of Charles, Earl of Lennox, in 1576, that Bishop Robert decided, belatedly, to enter into matrimony, which he did on 1578/9 at the age of about fifty-five. His bride was Elizabeth, daughter of the Earl of Atholl and widow of Lord Lovat. She obtained a divorce on 19 May 1581, ostensibly on the grounds of impotence, but the true reason seems to have been that she wanted urgently to marry James Stewart, Earl of Arran, which she did on 6 July. It may seem odd that a man who stood as close to the throne as Robert Stewart did, and who seems in some ways to have earned respect, played so little part in politics. One contemporary called him 'simple',[58] but one wonders if he did not show a good deal of common sense in preferring to enjoy his books and his golf at St Andrews; he almost deserved a prize for survival. He died on 29 August 1586.

Whatever the emphasis in his life, there was no doubt as to the emphasis at his death. He was buried, and commemorated with one of those handsome tombs characteristic of the period, in the quiet chapel of St Leonard in St Andrews, only a few feet away from the grave of John Winram, subprior of St Andrews and, so his tombstone says, 'Episcopus Fifanorum', Bishop of the people of Fife. Only about a dozen men, each in his own region, played a prominent active part in the initial organisation of the reformed ministry. It is appropriate that two of them rest together in the primatial city.

ROBERT STEWART AND HIS KINSFOLK

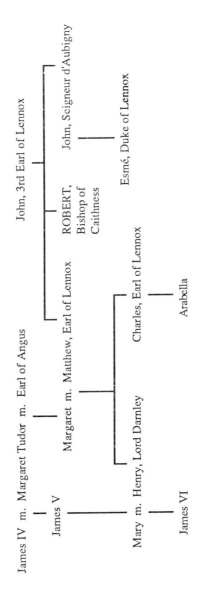

1   *Letters of James V,* 370, 432. The third edition of the *Handbook of British Chronology* omits the second of the two Andrews.
2   *Scottish Antiquary,* vi, 137.
3   The Rental of Caithness is in EUL MS Dc. 4.43, fo. 106; The Collectors' Accounts are of course printed (*TB*).
4   *Letters of James V,* 370, 432; *St Andrews Formulare,* ii, no.415.
5   Keith, i, 87.
6   *Epistolae Regum Scottorum,* ii, 222-3.
7   *RSS,* iii, 1267.
8   *APS,* ii, 452, 454-6.
9   *St Andrews Formulare,* ii, no.532.
10 *L & P,* xxi, i, 248, 323.
11 Ibid,., xix, ii, 442.
12 I am indebted to Miss A M Oakley, Archivist at Canterbury Cathedral, City and Diocesan Record Office, for giving me extracts of the entries relating to Robert Stewart (Reg. U, fos. 143v, 193v-194) and for information about the statutes.
13 *L & P,* xxi, i, 287, 470, 471, 493.
14 Ibid., i, 618, ii, 43.
15 *RSS,* iii, 2561.
16 *Public Affairs,* 553-4; Acts of the Lords of Council and Session (CS6), xxi, 115.
17 *Public Affairs,* 577; ADC et Sess., xxiv, 169, xxv, 32.
18 Mey Papers, 48, 50.
19 SRO, Yule Collection (GD90/3/11). I am indebted to Mr John Ballantyne for this item.
20 *RSS,* iv, 883, 1372.
21 Books of Sederunt, i, 35v; Fraser, *Sutherland,* iii, 124; *Scottish Antiquary,* vi, 137; Mey Papers, 79; *RMS,* iv, 697.
22 *DNB.*
23 *Scottish Antiquary,* xii, 2.
24 *Origines Parochiales,* II, ii (from Sutherland Charters).
25 Pitcairn, i, *337.
26 *PSAS,* xi, 87 et seq.
27 Mey Papers, 48-9.
28 Fraser, *Sutherland,* iii, 124.
29 W. Douglas Simpson, ed., *The Viking Congress* (1954), 230-38.
30 Mey Papers, 79, 81.
31 *CSP, Scot,* i, 575.
32 *BUK,* i, 222.
33 Mey Papers, 65-68, 70.
34 *RSS,* ii, 4946, iii, 2228, 2353, 2717.
35 *BUK,* i, 34.
36 Ibid., 130.
37 Ibid., 189-90.
38 *RMS,* v, 561.
39 *OP.,* ii, 617, 723.
40 SRO, Misc. Charters (RH 13/3), 84.
41 *Earls of Sutherland,* 150-51.
42 *OP,* ii, 617, 723; cf. *RSS,* v, 2466.
43 *APS,* iii, 23 c. 7.
44 *BUK,* i, 130.
45 Ibid., 104.
46 *TB.,* 208.
47 *RSS,* vii, 1788.

48   *SHS Misc.*, i, pp. xl-xlix.
49   James Melville, *Autobiography and Diary*, 126.
50   *St Andrews Kirk Session Register* (SHS), see index s.v. Caithness.
51   *RSS*, vi, 1473-4, 2309, vii, 789.
52   *Historical Catalogue of Scottish Bishops*, ed. M. Russell, 216.
53   E.g., *RSS*, vi, 1551, 1562, 1579, 1676, 1811.
54   *RSS*, viii, 887.
55   *Scott. Antiq.*, vi, 138.
56   *Early Scottish Music Consort* (Saltire Soc., 1984), 7.
57   Donaldson, *The First Trial of Mary, Queen of Scots*, 119.
58   *Scots Peerage*, v, 355.

INDEX